the other worlds

OFFBEAT ADVENTURES OF A CURIOUS TRAVELER

TOM MATTSON

DUDLEY COURT PRESS
SONOITA, AZ

Published in the United States of America by Dudley Court Press
PO Box 102 Sonoita, AZ 85637
www.DudleyCourtPress.com

FRONT COVER PHOTO CREDIT: Tom Mattson.
On the trail through Tiger Leaping Gorge in China, close to Tibet. 2006.
BACK COVER AUTHOR PHOTO: Thomas Leonard Studio, *thomasleonardstudio.com*.
COVER AND INTERIOR DESIGN: Dunn+Associates, www.Dunn-Design.com

Publisher's Cataloging-in-Publication Data
Mattson, Tom, 1945- author.
The other worlds : offbeat adventures of a curious traveler / Tom Mattson.
Description: Sonoita, AZ ; Dudley Court Press, [2020]
Identifiers: ISBN: 978-1-940013-63-3 (paperback) | 978-1-940013-64-0 (ebook)
978-1-940013-65-7 (audio) | LCCN: 2019917558
Subjects: Mattson, Tom, 1945- —Travel. | Travelers' writings, American.
Americans—Foreign countries—Anecdotes. | Voyages and travels—Anecdotes.
Adventure and adventurers—Anecdotes. | American essays—21st century. | LCGFT: Travel writing.
BISAC: TRAVEL / General. | TRAVEL / Essays & Travelogues. | TRAVEL / Special Interest / Adventure.
BIOGRAPHY & AUTOBIOGRAPHY / Adventurers & Explorers.
LCC: G465 | DDC: 910.4/1—dc23

Look for other books in this series at your favorite bookseller
or at www.DudleyCourtPress.com

I dedicate this book

to the people I've met around the world,

some of whom make bold appearances in the stories I write.

They range from Maribel in Havana—the first story—

to the Dani people in a New Guinea village—

near the conclusion, as well as Minnesotans,

who pop up by surprise.

CUBA, CANADA, and the UNITED STATES

AROUND THE WORLD IN 400 DAYS

MESOAMERICA

ASIA: 2006 and 2010

NEW YORK CITY and LONDON

HOMEBOUND

NOTES IN BOTTLES

THE SLOW GOODBYES

ACKNOWLEDGEMENTS

Dan MacMeekin, a late and dear friend to so many, encouraged me from the start, beginning with my first brief message in 2004. Over the years, he forwarded to me motivating comments from among the two dozen readers with whom he shared my writings. Through Dan, I've met Bob Distad and Linda Messenger, and corresponded with Patricia Simoni near the East Coast, as well as poet-writer Andy Anderson on the West Coast—all of whom I thank for their comments over the years. And I greatly appreciate Andy's astute evaluation of the manuscript.

I'm also indebted to others whose reactions and feelings about my periodic missives from the road meant I had to commit myself to being word-active and thought-creative whenever opportunities came my way. They include my brother James Mattson, sister Mary Elieisar, niece and grandniece Ailina and Reneé Mattson, Joan Felciano, and Leah White, as well as Alice Lundblad and Hisako Matsuda, whose support never wavered, even past their 100th birthdays.

Keeping my writing engine running, too, were Tom and Jo Nemanick, Ron and Betty Anzelc, and Jerry and Jeannie Newton. Special thanks to 91-year-old Don Purkat, a World War II Navy veteran who served in the South Pacific and a lifelong resident of the village closest to my home, a tiny mining town that could perish under the weight of an expanding iron mine. Don instigated the publication of three stories in Hometown Focus, and I've hand-delivered many more to his house since then.

Encouragement and advice have also come from younger readers. Asa, a budding entrepreneur, tells me he "can't wait" until the book is

ACKNOWLEDGMENTS

in his hands, so he can read my stories. I suggested he start with the tale of my being lost in a pitch-black barn with a pig in China. He'll have to get a little reading help from his mother, for he has just turned seven. And my cousins Alyson and Nick Maki, twins who just turned nine, helpfully suggested book titles. They've listened to some of my adventures and, as good readers, will soon have a new book to explore.

Further afield, I've received valuable comments from Kimpei Ohara, Tom Woxland, Mel Martynn, Lee Mattson, Dave Fadness, Cindy Bertheau, Eva Hertzer, Janet Econome, Dave Collins, and Richard Ochs. And from world explorers Kathie Feig and Bob Young, and global sailors of years past, Judy Knape and Bryan Lane.

Like many other authors, I'm indebted to my friend David Setnicker for his invaluable insights and advice on writing and publishing. Larry and Irene Chance conquered heavily marked up drafts and diligently deciphered my revisions at their computers, while providing very welcome insights and comments.

A huge thank you to Gail Woodard of Dudley Court Press, which published this book. Without Gail's keen interest, advice and amazing grasp of publishing, my stories would be biding their time, unfinished. Gail's online seminars have also been of great value to me, as has the expert work of Gail's production assistant Teresa Evans. I am also indebted to copy editor Pam Nordberg. All are top-flight professionals.

I have been favored by the incredible and unsurpassed talent in cover and book design of Kathi Dunn of Dunn + Associates. Their work is on display in this book—on the front and back covers and on every page in between.

Superb editor Caroline Lambert proved to me what magic a great professional like her can perform on one's writings, even after they've already seen years of labor. It is magic I believe in, but only because I've seen it at work. Graphic Designer Lori Thompson of W.A. Fisher expertly took charge of the maps in this book. After poring over hundreds of maps during decades of travel, these are the first in which

I'm a player—albeit a decidedly dreamy one in the Grain of Salt Map! Thank you, Don Peterson, owner of Thomas Leonard Studio, for your wonderful photographs, including the shot of me and my globe. My gratitude also goes to Barb Tucker and Ian Carlson of Andrews Cameras, who offered expert technical assistance.

The public library staff in the city of Virginia, and those in other Iron Range towns, may not have known what I had up my sleeve when I first started all these years ago, but without their assistance and the libraries' modern technology, I'd still be at square one with this book.

And I may still be at square one or square 1.5 in life if it weren't for newspapers, and in particular, The Biwabik Times. While in my teens, publishers Roy and Katy Coombe taught me the science and art of reporting on local government meetings, selling advertising, running presses, melting linotype metal, taking and developing photographs, and setting headlines by hand. What an opportunity for a kid! The evidence is all around us that the world is a giving place.

INTRODUCTION

None of it was meant to be: the stories and anecdotes that appear in this book, my travels to far-flung other worlds, being face-to-face with hundreds of strangers. Yet here we are, and there I've been, and somehow, strangers became friends.

I'm at this juncture in life, just as others are at theirs, because of many chance happenings, experiences and forks in the road.

Yet as I trace back the meandering road that brought me here today, I can see where it all started many years ago. As luck had it, I caught the travel bug when I was still a child. I first traveled with my family from Minnesota to Canada in a 1940s Chevrolet to visit cousins from the old country, Finland. We then traveled by Greyhound Bus to visit my mother's brothers, who'd moved to California. In Hollywood, we chatted with Debbie Reynolds and Art Linkletter. And at Tennessee Ernie Ford's radio show, we heard his first performance of the song Sixteen Tons ("and what do you get?"). "That song will be a hit!" my mother claimed right after the show. I scoffed. Capitol Records seemed to agree with me: it released Sixteen Tons on the B side of a record. DJs proceeded to play the B side only, and that song sold two million copies in two months. How do mothers know?

Could we keep the family traveling show moving? Yes, we could. We ventured to Monterrey, Mexico, to World Fairs in Seattle and New York City, and to the halls of Congress in Washington D.C.—where we stepped back against a wall in a narrow corridor, allowing soon-to-be-elected JFK and LBJ to pass by, smiles all around.

Sometime later, it was Haight-Asbury, 1967-style, with my friend Ron. After experiencing a bit of that Summer of Love in San Francisco and growing more mature by the week, I felt I was ready to travel on my own.

Yet I still had not picked up a pen to write.

The first travel experience mentioned in this book came a year after the Summer of Love, back in California, when I told myself, "I've dreamed about hopping freight trains, and I will!" How did that turn out? A Note in a Bottle, later in this book, will take you riding those California rails with me.

And here I am, many years, countries and chance encounters later.

"What is your favorite country?" I've been asked from Minnesota to Kanazawa, Japan.

"Don't ask such a difficult question," I might say.

A much easier question is the less common, "Why do you love traveling so?"

"The people I meet, the surprises, the unknowns, the challenges," I declare. And I may add, "I meet people by chance, and every person is a treasure to behold. The smile, laugh, energy, determination, dreams and pain. And each person's own world of family, friends, play—and stories."

As I prepared the manuscript for this book, I visited or wrote to many of these people. They were intrigued and embraced my re-telling their stories to you. By luck, I've met Maribel on the same park bench in Havana several times over the years. From that very park, she observed towering historical figures of the 20th Century. She is just as pleased to have her stories told to you as she was in telling them to me.

I first met Ou Gong Hua in a village in China. He appears several times in this book, stretching over a decade. "I hope to get the book when it is published," he has told me. "I am very happy that I can be a story, and I want to see the stories of you and others."

Chema, a Maya fisherman who lives on the shores of 1,200-foot-deep Lake Atitlan in Guatemala, beamed with surprise and pride as we discussed his story appearing in a book. For years, unbeknownst to him, I'd written about bits of his life in messages to friends. All this time, I'd known him only by his nickname, Chema. But he told me he wants people who read about his life to know his full five-part name. I agreed and am happy to know it myself now: Jose Maria Mardoqueo Cotuc Hernandez.

"Sharing one's stories with the world brings greater value to one's life and experiences," Erin Thormodsgard of Miles City, Montana reflected, as we talked about the reactions of Maribel, Ou Gong Hua and Chema. As I rode off from Erin's eclectic shop and coffeehouse on my motorcycle, I think I could hear what my friends, once strangers, were urging me to do: Make my story travel!

Page by page, I hope you feel, as I do, that people out there in the other worlds are, at their core, so much like you and me; they are ever so fascinating and have so much to offer. And, I feel, we are eager to receive.

So, let us begin.

CUBA,
CANADA,
and the
UNITED
STATES

CUBA

The Shots Maribel Heard

APRIL 6, 2014

I'm your guy in Havana. I scribbled down a story for you. Here it is, unscribbled.

First, the preconceptions. It is 10:30 a.m. There is an elderly woman —a bit older than me—sitting on the park bench. She doesn't read or do much of anything at all. So I doubt she would have anything interesting, much less enlightening, to tell me. After all, she just gazes ahead, a faded white plastic bag on her lap. In her bag might be fresh government-subsidized bread and a fruit or vegetable from a new free-market cart wheeled on the streets.

I catch her glancing a couple times at my three-month-old *New York Times*, bought near New York's Central Park once upon a time. I decide I'll get up now and leave with a simple parting expression.

Before I can utter *adios*, the silent woman speaks. "What time is it?" she asks in Spanish.

I'm a slow reader, and by now it's 11:30 a.m. I tell her.

"Where are you from?" she then asks.

"I'm from the United States of America. Minnesota," I answer.

"It's cold there," she continues, still in Spanish.

She wouldn't know any English, of course, I tell myself. I point at a photo in the newspaper and inform her it pictures New York's winter —"it is ice on a bay." She looks at the English caption. It shows "Rio Hudson," she tells me. Not a bay.

I read the photo caption with more care. Standing corrected, I decide to ask her a thing or two. I find out that the nearly silent woman studied English with an American teacher many years ago, but she doesn't speak it anymore. She remembers how to read some words, though, like "Hudson River." She's lived in this neighborhood around Havana's Parque Central all her life, and she's traveled Cuba far and wide. She's a member of one of the Spanish societies in Cuba, since her parents were from Spain. She went there once with her father, she says.

Now she unties her large plastic bag. Inside is another plastic bag. She unties that one, and then another inside it. She withdraws an item and holds it up for me to see. It's her Spanish passport. She puts it back in the small plastic bag. I ask if she has a Cuban passport. She reopens the small bag and withdraws her Cuban passport. Other small bags remain tantalizingly unopened.

A man hobbles by and asks for a peso. I tell him I don't have any. He then asks for a pen. I don't have any of those, either. "He doesn't

Havana, near Parque Central and Maribel's park bench. El Capitolio looms in the background.

have any," she tells him. "He has," the man says in Spanish as he departs. Her facial expression is dismissive. What her face and her hands communicate is just as absorbing as her words.

"Has the economy improved and your life changed the last few years?" I venture to ask. She shakes her head, waves her forearm a few inches, and studies my face to see if I got her message. I think she knows I won't say a word (except an unscribbled one to you). Cubans have been less reticent to be critical the last two or three years.

"Do you remember when Fulgencio Batista was the leader of Cuba?" I ask.

"Yes. I'd see him, his wife, and his family riding around these streets in a car."

"Do you remember the assault on Batista's Presidential Palace in 1957?"

"Yes," she says. "There were gunshots everywhere. You can still see bullet holes in the building over there. You can see dozens more in the Presidential Palace. My father didn't let me go out of the apartment. I only heard all the shooting." Of the 39 members of the student-led assault team, 36 were shot dead in the failed attempt to overthrow the corrupt dictator. "I didn't see Batista riding around in the streets after that," she tells me.

"Did you see Fidel Castro riding around in the streets?"

"Yes," she answers. "He was riding around within two years. And Che Guevara drove around alone in his Jeep. As the leader, Fidel always had bodyguards."

Seeing that I was excited to learn about her sightings of historic figures, she brings up another. "I used to see Ernest Hemingway walking on these streets. He always went to the bar El Floridita, right over there on Obispo Street. He had a beard. He wore a T-shirt and shorts and had sandals the same color as the ones I'm wearing now. He was so suntanned. And huge!"

She points out the art deco Bacardi Building over there, the remarkable art museum right over here, and a huge mansion formerly owned by a family who fled Cuba and now, seemingly, being renovated for a hotel. She reopens her bag of bags and carefully draws out a paper. It is her church's program of events for Holy Week. "I am a Catholic," she wants me to know.

I realize, again, that I've never met anyone I can't learn something from. Don't prejudge an elderly woman sitting silently on a park bench with a plastic bag on her lap.

"What is your name?" I ask the woman on the marble bench.

"My name is Maribel."

I slide *The New York Times* and a peso over to her, both of which she values. "I hope we meet in this park tomorrow," I tell Maribel as I head off to the bullet-riddled Presidential Palace, now the Museum of the Revolution.

"Yes," Maribel answers. "Tomorrow."

Why Do You Love the Other Worlds So?
MARCH 1, 2010 AT 6:07 PM

Hi Charles,

In Havana, I planted my feet for three hours on the 1580, standing-room-only, stone floor of the Basilica of San Francisco at a concert of classical singers. Many of the performers were students or alumni of the National School of the Arts, the famed institute conceived by Fidel and Che on Cuba's ritziest golf course, abandoned by golfers who fled after the revolution. The school trains young Cubans and many from the developing world in ballet, modern dance, visual arts, music, and theater.

One night, I met three strangers on a street a few blocks from the basilica and imbibed rum with them in an ancient apartment up four staircases, surrounded by Afro-Cuban Santería offerings and statues. They invited me to make my own offering in which I could, and did, remember family and friends.

Now in Cienfuegos ("one hundred fires"), I have my room from last year in a 1959 "California suburban home" designed by a notable architect. Called Casa Juanchi, it's owned by Juan Sanchez and his wife Norma. They maintain the original furnishings and park a white 1957 Chevy in the driveway. In the lush backyard, I've been reading *One Hundred Years of Solitude* by Columbian Nobel novelist Gabriel García Márquez, a book Norma read in this house years ago. Now I'll have supper downtown, 40 blocks from my suburban home.

MARCH 1, 2010, 9:09 PM

Dear Tom,

I took the time to look up your location on the interweb and imagine myself on Cuba's south shore, absorbing the white, pillared architecture of the Cuban city of a hundred fires.

I can tell that you enjoy the foreign culture. It seems most other travelers would do the same. *Why do you love the other worlds so, Tom?*

No mind to the vacancy duration of messages from one another. I accept that time is short for both of us.

Venture well, Charles

MARCH 30, 2010

Hello Charles,

You've looked up the spots I visit! My friend Ed said he does that too.

"Why do you love the other worlds so?" you asked. You're the first person to pose that question to me. Here's what I recently told the youngest American (18) that I've met traveling alone in strange countries:

Trillions of planets are spaced out inside our universe, and a new theory says there might be a number of universes. Our planet is so diverse, amazing, and surprising that even God, perhaps, could not have dreamt it up. Through the quarter million or so years of human history, very few people have had the opportunity to explore different parts of the planet. Even today, only a tiny percentage of us have that chance. The book of exploration is right in front of us, and we've opened it. You and I move from one page to the next.

Well, Charles, the book is interactive, and the traveler can add a little to each page, though usually you can't delete or revise what's already embedded. The pages are fascinating to behold: they're in color, emit smells, are three dimensional and can be touched, and most everything on the pages is moving.

Anything new, Charles, on the January, February, and March pages in the book of wonder that you are experiencing and helping to write?

• • •

Years after this interchange with Charles—on January 1, 2019, to be exact—I discovered in a dusty attic box a forgotten aerogramme sent from Nepal. I'd received it in my hometown of Biwabik, Minnesota, in 1972. I'd forgotten the sender's name, but there it was: Tim Clark, a Peace Corp volunteer.

Tim had engineered a trek for me and himself into the remote Himalayas—and then sent me deeper yet on my own with a hand-scribbled map and a bare handful of words in Nepali that might see me through.[1]

Now, in 2019, just before the ink on Tim's 1972 aerogramme letter would fade into unwritten history, I read his message for the second time in my life. Schoolteacher Tim presciently seemed to answer Charles's question, "Why do you love the other worlds so?"

[1] For more on Tim, witness his bold appearance in "Around the World in 400 Days."

I talk after school [with my Nepali family] about interesting, peculiar discoveries of the day. Like everyone's name has a meaning, or the relative order of castes, or what happens when people die, or when they will plant corn again, or how to set a broken arm, or when will supper be ready tonight. And none of it is as strange as the memory that I used to ride a freeway to college every morning.

Concluding his letter, Tim wrote:

A question for you, Tom: is the sense of wonder, the ingenious questions you ask, a part of you, like the color of your hair, or did you learn that? I'd like to know your answer. Tom, I'd also be really interested on how you get on in America.

Your friend, Tim

The answers I sent Tim have faded away, and the words may be buried in the high Himalayas—perhaps to be discovered by another curious traveler.

A Village in the Mountains
APRIL 21, 2014

Soon, when I return to Minnesota and fix my first breakfast, please understand if I amble in the yard looking *loco*. I might be searching for guava and orange trees to make juice, for bananas to concoct a side dish, and for sun-dried coffee beans from hills this side of yonder. A nearby garden should have red peppers for the omelet. And where is that nearby stream with bubbling fresh water?

My mind will be harking back to Santo Domingo, a mountain village a mile long and two lazy riverbanks wide. The village is in Cuba's

Sierra Maestra Mountains, which look south over the Caribbean toward Jamaica. Sharply up from Santo Domingo, Fidel Castro built his secret command post in 1958, and *campesinos* from town were tortured by Fulgencio Batista's soldiers searching for the elusive revolutionaries. Blood was shed—including the blood of my friend Juan's grandfather.

If you go to Santo Domingo, have travel guru Anley Rosales Benitez taxi you from Bayamo, then bed down in a cabin near Ulises's casa, which welcomes travelers who make it here. It's known as Casa Sierra Maestra and is set along the River Yara, where you can find a swimming hole upriver. Go to bed at 9 p.m. Cover up for the 55-degree daybreak temperature—this is the coolest village in Cuba.

In this cabin last night, I dreamt I could have the very breakfast I've just described 365 mornings a year, every year. For $2.25, Ulises's family will place your table outdoors under a flowery canopy, in a spot warmed by the first sunrays cresting over the mountain. They'll also make you lunch and dinner. Throw in the one-room cabin for $20 a night—less if you'll stay a couple years, which I was about to do in my dream. You and Ulises can work this out. Or stay just three or four days at a time, three years in a row, and he'll say you broke my own record of "foreigner who comes the most and stays the longest."

Lose yourself in the rocking chair on the tilting veranda. The floor is only one thing that tilts left hereabouts. That the cabin door can never shut, day or night, is inconsequential. Call a shack a shack if you're so inclined. The place does sport a fan and a light bulb, though. By the time you arrive, the village will have a cell phone antenna if all goes right. Ulises is thinking about getting a phone, but he's not sure. If he never gets one, you'll have to come and ask him about the village in person. Population of Santo Domingo? Two hundred. Horses? Sixty. Cars locally owned? Zero.

During your stay in Santo Domingo, you may have it in your head to ask for Lucas Castillo's old house, just upriver from the cabin you've already decided to commandeer. You'll find that the old house is now a museum. Peer at the fading maps that display the rebel and army offensives and counterthrusts. Don't fall into the gaping holes in the floor—though if you do, a military cot might catch you.

In 1928, Lucas, an enterprising young man, fled harsh economic realities in the lowlands. He found unfarmed land running from the River Yara up the steep mountains. By the 1950s, Lucas and his wife were cultivating fields and hills of corn, rice, coffee, yucca, mangoes, and papayas. Their grandson Juan lived with them.

Toward the end of the decade, the Sierra Maestra Mountains were teeming with rebels, led by the likes of Fidel Castro, his brother Raúl, and Che Guevara. They built their secluded *La Comandancia* up the mountains from Santo Domingo. From this secret camp, they planned the last 18 months of the revolution that would eventually topple the entrenched dictator.

What the rebels new to these mountains needed were weapons, medical supplies, and—most of all—food. Lucas had an almost endless supply of nutritious produce. He and others spirited tons of it to the rebels. His actions were incredibly risky, especially since an ever more nervous Batista had now dispatched 10,000 troops to the mountains. Grandson Juan and many villagers fled, surviving in caves and on mountain slopes for 45 days. Meanwhile, the dictator's forces found Lucas in Santo Domingo. They tortured and murdered him (and soon killed six more villagers). Batista's army then took over Lucas's house, digging holes through the floor into the ground for protection against rebel attacks. When the tide turned against Batista, grandson Juan returned home. He found his grandfather's body, his torso punctured by bayonets.

Yesterday, I had the good fortune of visiting Juan, who is now 65. He, his wife Maria, and family members live close to his grandfather's old house, now the museum with a Batista army cot plugging up a

Juan Castillo (left) at his Santo Domingo doorway in the historic Sierra Maestra Mountains. In the pivotal year of 1958, Juan met Fidel Castro, Che Guevara, and other revolutionaries as they made battle plans at his childhood home a stone's throw from here. Juan's son Miguel (right) is a mountain guide.

hole in the floor. We talked baseball, iced-up Minnesota lakes, and eyewitnessing a revolution as an eight-year-old. Juan is one of the few still here today who saw, in flesh and blood, Fidel Castro and Che Guevara waging a revolution against all odds. I caught the wince of pain in Juan's eyes when we discussed the summer of 1958. By the end of that year, Batista had fled the country without ever finding the *Comandancia*, despite a 10,000 to 300 troop advantage.

Today, Juan's son Miguel is a mountain guide based on the edge of Santo Domingo. Miguel (or a co-guide) leads visitors on hikes through Fidel's expansive command center up a steep mountain road. Under a remote canopy of trees, Fidel's old cabin is still there, untouched. Everyone except a guard must depart this old post by sundown. I have to admit that I've started dreaming of a way to stay in Fidel's cabin, maybe for a week. Shameful, I know. But that would be to die for.

Shortly before his murder by Batista's forces in 1958, Lucas found a government army bayonet on the ground. He gave it to his grandson Juan, who still has it and offered to show it to me. The bayonet had remained hidden for so long that Juan and his wife couldn't locate it at first. They grew worried as they searched the rooms and the property. After awhile, Juan, bayonet in hand, marched into the living room where I was waiting in a rocking chair. The weapon carries the number 1911, letters, and a symbol, a relic of the revolution.

I suggested that I photograph the markings and search for the bayonet's origin once I'm back in the USA. Juan was pleased, but seemed to wonder how I might actually go about it. I think it can be done, I said: I've found information about the World War II German Mauser rifle my Uncle Ernie picked up in Europe in 1945 and gave me for deer hunting. Employing some internet magic, I discovered that my Mauser was originally fitted with a bayonet, but it's long been lost.

I hope to be armed with information about that special Cuban bayonet when I return to the cabin along the River Yara, seeking 100 years of solitude.

Che's Mausoleum or Bar La Roca?
MARCH 26, 2015

the first part

I've ducked into the Hotel Santa Clara Libre lobby to use its computer. I'm gazing out the windows at Santa Clara's grand central plaza. Last night, on the other side of the plaza, I found aging plaques commemorating heroic Cubans. I learned that in 1959, just days after the revolutionary victory over Fulgencio Batista, Fidel Castro addressed crowds here. Shortly before that, Che Guevara had won a pivotal clash in Santa Clara, ingeniously derailing a two-locomotive armored train carrying 373 of Batista's heavily armed soldiers. No wonder this town is now called the "city of the heroic guerillas."

Meeting you this morning as we slowly circled the plaza's band stand in opposite directions pleased me greatly. Your first adventure to Cuba started just yesterday, you remarked, and came about quite by accident. I don't know the details. You enthused about seeing the boxcars, still derailed, 15 blocks from here. You mentioned you've seen photos posted all over the internet under "Che *Tren Blindado.*" You also visited the Che museum and stepped into "a cool and oh! so comfortable" mausoleum holding Che's remains and those of Cubans who fought and died with him in Bolivia.

You urged me to visit all these places. I'm thinking of doing that today, I said. Or perhaps, instead, I'll be paying a return visit to Bar La Roca ("The Rock"). I think I can still find it a dozen blocks away in a barrio whose name I never knew. I'll sit and order shots of rum; that's all they sell besides cigarettes and cigars. I've forgotten if the shots cost 5 cents or 10 cents, but I could let you know sometime. I daresay not a single photo of the bar has ever been posted on the internet. And never will be.

I need to decide real soon whether to go to La Roca or instead to the derailed train and Che's Mausoleum you recommended. "Will you please help me decide?" I ask you.

the fidgety part

I'm getting fidgety. Do I sense you are imagining the world inside Bar La Roca? I think the most historic mausoleum in the Americas and the derailed train that helped change the course of a nation will wait for me until tomorrow. Now, I think I hear your inner voice suggesting I invite *you* to La Roca.

So the bar is where we plan to spend an hour of our precious lives—or perhaps stay for a timeless forever. Let's walk to the barrio whose name we never knew.

the final part

In a surprise move at the doorway, I suggest you go into La Roca by yourself. You'll realize it's best appreciated without a fellow traveler.

You step inside and take five steps to the counter. You're one of the few going in without an empty pint-sized bottle in your back pocket. That means you'll do all your drinking here.

Order a double shot of rum for a couple coins worth less than 10 US cents. You'll likely decide there's no earthly reason to ever order a single shot.

Plunk yourself in one of five rickety chairs at one of only three miniscule tables. In come the street vendor and bill collector to have their empty bottles filled and perhaps to down a drink too. In comes the mechanic, his clothes oily from knees to chest, to order a double shot. In comes the painter, marked in a variety of colors from his shoes to his cap; he sits on a chair, and later on a different chair, and all the while he holds a six-inch-wide paintbrush in one hand. Dragging his big hoe into the bar, a farmer gets his bottle filled and strides out, the hoe slung over his shoulder. All the others, you don't know what they do, since you're not a regular just yet.

The bar has a capacity of six or eight for the busy stream and can hold two bicycles. The bicycles pushed in by its mobile clientele are ever changing. This one here has a machete tied down to the rear rack with two different colors of twine. Another has a homemade seat—child-sized and wooden—affixed on the cross bar. Hung from most bicycles' handlebars are bags of unknowns. The door is always open, but you barely remember there's a world out there, for heaven's sake.

An elderly man now squats down next to your table. His "On Time" brand undershorts are showing because his belt has missed the back loop of his pants. Rather than asking the most common question you get in Cuba ("Where are you from?"), he just points at you and exclaims, "*Italiano!*" You say "no" and name the country you're from (usually to a surprised, delighted look, like his).

A pack of cigarettes, you notice, costs 35 cents. Just one cig is priced proportionately at one-twentieth of that amount. If you've been craving a smoke for decades, it's all right to succumb in here. It will take you back to a time before the advent of filters, and certainly before those pure white filters, those Micronite filters, those recessed filters, and those off-color filters that caused strong cowboys to die early with their boots on.

When you're finished with your one smoke of the century (so far), flick the butt toward the floor drain. Or just let it drop to the floor of its own volition. It's all up to you. So many responsibilities. But so much time.

By now, you're imagining an earlier era. Fidel Castro and Che Guevara are regaling everyone in La Roca, expounding a brief history of the revolution that ended the day before yesterday.

In the middle of it all, go ahead and check out the bright sunshine on Naranjo Street for a few minutes. Just a quarter block away, admire a work of art—a rolling wooden cart with beautifully arranged vegetables and fruits, along with onions hanging on strings. It's one of the new private businesses authorized by the government.

Beside the cart, a young man sits on his bicycle. You tell him you've just been in Bar La Roca. His ballet of hand and facial expressions, tightly coordinated with a spit-out muttering, lets you know that he finds La Roca utterly disgusting. But you've got him right where you want him. Though you're not one to point fingers, you don't mince words, either: "Your bicycle was inside the bar but an hour ago," you point out.

"The bicycle belongs to my father," he explains with a bit of fidgeting.

Those under 40 don't flock to La Roca. It's for the seasoned, like you and me. The brightness of day is unforgiving, and now you escape from the blinding sun back inside the bar, where you might stay for an eternity. If you ever decide to leave, take a cue from others who've done so before you. Saunter up to the counter. Place your well-used plastic cup upside down or right side up. Or just toss it over. Whatever you do, you won't be out of line.

Next year, when I visit Santa Clara again, I'll glance through the door. I may see you on a rickety chair. When I hit the joint, I'll leave everything I know at the curb. Bar La Roca may well become the center of my universe, too.

Advance Man
HAVANA, CUBA
MARCH 15, 2016

President Barack Obama
The White House
Washington, D.C.

Dear Mr. President:
I am in Havana. I'm your man. My application has, I assume, been accepted. I overnighted it three hours after the White House announced your groundbreaking visit this coming Sunday. Two days later, my boots hit the ground. I've been reconnoitering since.

The American Embassy here has briefed you electronically on what it knows. My task—none ever too tall—is to fill in the cracks with nit and grit. Better the world remembers your visit for a century than just 25 years. Fasten your seatbelt. Here we go!

mass bedlam in Havana
First, reschedule your hour of arrival, please, or you'll mess up the arrival of hundreds of passengers flying from Toronto, Paris, and

Buenos Aires. Thanks to you, they're coming in droves to beat the Americans, who'll soon fill the rooms and send prices higher. Lines at Immigration are long. Even someone on a high-level mission like mine waited 90 minutes after touchdown for a checked backpack.

aerial maneuvers above Cuba

Here's the prescription to avoid mass bedlam upon your arrival. Lift off from Andrews Air Force Base at the scheduled time so no one suspects what's on the horizon. Once the navigator has got his bearings, instruct the cockpit to deviate left by 21 degrees, no questions asked. (For your convenience, I'll attach an *Eyes Only* map of Air Force One's revised route.) Yes, you'll first see Cuba down below at the eastern extremity that faces Haiti, and you'll be 539 miles off the specified course. But you're about to conduct a surprise aerial surveillance for the ages, equaling the Air Force U2 spy plane flights that discovered Soviet nuclear-tipped missiles almost ready to strike major American cities in October 1962.

Down below, admire Baracoa, the only city near Cuba's eastern tip and the first settlement in the country founded by Europeans. (Hundreds of advanced native communities had been thriving for many centuries, every last one wiped out rather quickly once Cuba was "discovered.")

Baracoa will celebrate its 505th anniversary this August. Townsfolk will later proclaim that if they knew you were flying above, they'd have hauled the old wooden cross out into the plaza—the cross everyone says Columbus carried ashore. Angling west-southwest, in eight minutes you'll be over Guantánamo, where yet more evidence of torture under your predecessor was again published in the paper here last week.

After a couple gulps of water and a Tylenol to deal with the Guantánamo headache, look down on Santiago. This is where, among thousands of US fighters, Teddy Roosevelt and the Rough Riders stormed up San Juan Hill against the Spanish in 1898, thinking boots in stirrups and elsewhere would forever cement Cuba as a US ally.

Next, gaze at the horizon on the right. You'll get a glimpse of the Castro family's once expansive farm, most of it expropriated after the revolution. Eldest brother Ramón, who had farmed it as Fidel went off to college and law school, died two weeks ago, age 91. The Castros do not die young.

Four minutes straight ahead, you won't have any trouble spotting Pico Turquino, especially if you skim the treetops. This is Cuba's tallest peak. A hair-raising 30 seconds later, you'll be right over one of the most historic revolutionary locations in the Americas: Fidel Castro's secret command post, Comandancia de La Plata. Dictator Fulgencio Batista could never find it in these tree-covered Sierra Maestra Mountains. La Comandancia is worth a few more words later in this report, but for now, be satisfied with *buzzing the hideout with Air Force One, one-upping Batista's Air Force!*

Moving along the southern coast, yours will be the first American plane not to get shot at over the Bay of Pigs, scene of the CIA-sponsored invasion to overthrow Fidel Castro. A building down on Playa Giron is now the Museum of the Bay of Pigs, made possible by a learn-as-you-go predecessor of yours in 1961. The exhibition is more educational than Miami's Bay of Pigs Museum, set up by the losing side. (You can, however, hear from a veteran or two in Miami of their trying to escape after the defeat, stumbling for days across hot and nasty terrain and killing a lizard just for hydration. And finally, capture!)

By now, the cockpit crew and international reporters aboard will have taken to your navigational orders. They'll applaud your call to jig back north-northeast, excited about what's next: Santa Clara. When you hear the Fox News reporter call for ambulances, explain that the sight of overturned railcars down there is really a page out of the history books. These are the remains of Batista's armored train (tren blindado), whose derailment Che Guevara engineered on December 28, 1958. Inside the boxcars were hundreds of soldiers armed to the teeth and provisions for two months. Within two weeks, however, Fidel Castro and the revolutionaries strode victoriously into Havana.

In 20 seconds, you'll fly over the tall statue of Che, which, at that time of day, should cast a shadow of his likeness right over his mausoleum. Tip your wing to Che. The only people in Santa Clara who won't look up in awe are those (of us) downing shots of rum in Bar La Roca.

Now it is on to Havana, Mr. President, the setting of you-count-'em-up assassination plots against Castro. Your fingers-on-the-trigger predecessors wanted him dead young. You are here on a different mission.

As you glide toward the airport, you'll see Havana Bay, where the USS Maine exploded and sank under mysterious circumstances in 1898. "Remember the Maine, and to hell with Spain"? No? Almost no one does. The last sitting American president to visit Cuba sailed into that very bay. Calvin Coolidge. 1928. On a battleship.

On March 20, 2016, Air Force One will land 80 minutes late, just as this report advises: during a lull in the incoming flights filled with Canadian, European, and South American tourists.

72 ice cream cones vs. 3

I am attaching a self-erasing map so you can retrace my steps through the airport. You'll find a new, look-back-over-your-shoulder spot for changing your dollars. You'll get 90 pesos for $100, rather than the rigid rate of 87 pesos. Then change a small handful of these pesos (called CUC) into the *other* kind of Cuban pesos (called pesos cubanos). At 24 to 1, you'll get 72 pesos cubanos if you hand over three CUC. I call it the Big Money and the Small Money.

Many tourists don't get the Small Money pesos used for some super-local transactions, like a soft ice cream cone. So when they see a posted price of one peso for the cone, they think it's the Big Money peso price. That equals about one US dollar. They pay it with a smile. But if you've changed some Big Money for Small Money, hand over one Small Money peso, about five US cents. You could buy five cones a day for five cents each and smile every time.

Keep Small Money pesos handy in your pocket, next to your Blackberry phone. A cup of coffee costs 1.5 US cents in Bayamo at Cafeteria Oriental. Supper at La Perla in Camagüey will be $1.60, followed by a Sonday Supremo at the Coppelia ice cream parlor for 12 cents. A bus ride in Cienfuegos is one cent. A double shot of rum at Bar La Roca in Santa Clara is 12 cents.

the mausoleum or the rum bar?

Last year, a story titled *Che's Mausoleum or Bar La Roca?* chronicled the dilemma of a foreign traveler: should he go to Che's mausoleum— cool, dimly lit, and oh so comfortable—or must he pay a repeat visit to Bar La Roca?

Those of us in the know will be angling to live out our old age within a bicycle ride of La Roca. You and I might meet there frequently, downing shots at our respective paces and sneaking in an occasional 2-cent cigarette—nonfilter, of course. We'll be in much good company. We all might close up the joint early some afternoon if the 60-gallon rum drum goes dry.

the shots she heard

You'll cruise toward Havana's Parque Central and the nearby El Capitolio in the big black Cadillac you fly around the world with you. In your first term, that car and its body double made striking appearances in a Central American story titled "A Journey to See Two Presidents." It's unpublished, but I may send it to you.

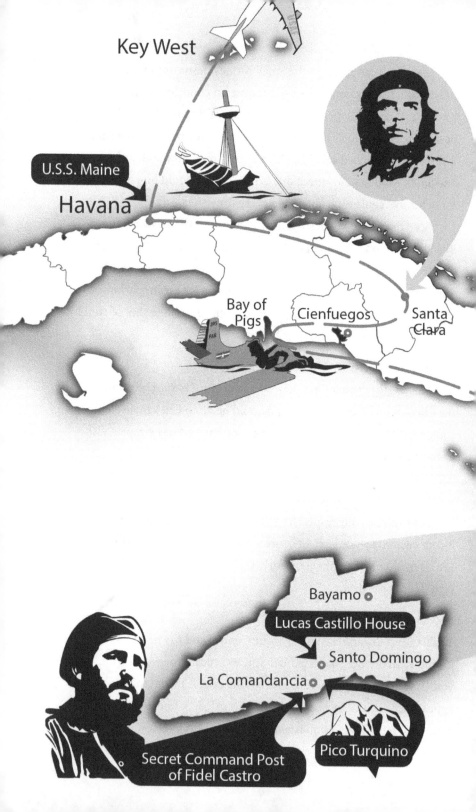

Key West

U.S.S. Maine

Havana

Bay of
Pigs

Cienfuegos

Santa
Clara

Bayamo

Lucas Castillo House

Santo Domingo

La Comandancia

Pico Turquino

Secret Command Post
of Fidel Castro

Just after you whiz by the majestic El Capitolio—resembling the American counterpart where you served four years as United States Senator—you need to step out of your limousine. Walk briskly ahead of your surprised (again) security detail, moving diagonally across Parque Central. I'm attaching a disappearing map leading you to the marble bench where you must sit down next to Maribel. You might ask, and she'll tell, about walking this neighborhood as a girl and seeing Ernest Hemingway, Fulgencio Batista, and a little later, Fidel Castro and Che Guevara.

Earlier this week I talked to Maribel about your visit starting Sunday, whispering to her that you'll have a map taking you right to her bench. She forewarned me: "They'll never let President Obama get out of his car and walk through the park. Crowds will gather. *They'll touch him.*" Please do it, though, and be touched by Maribel. Before you get up, steal a look back over your right shoulder. There, on the ground behind the trash barrel, you'll see a well-worn manila folder. It contains more intelligence. I left it yesterday. No one saw. It has your name on it.

the hotel California

Squeeze in a visit to the Museum of the Revolution, down El Prado a few blocks from Maribel's park. The museum was once the Presidential Palace and home to Batista—no wonder the outside walls are pitted with 1950s bullet holes fired by urban guerilla students and workers. Just inside you'll see a couple dozen more holes in the white marble wall. Visitors have stuck a finger in them and found out some are an inch deep. You may know that Batista escaped an assassination attempt by fleeing through a secret passageway from his second-floor office.

Let the lobby guard know you are from the United States. You probably remember how to say that in Spanish—*"Soy de Estados Unidos."* The guard will insist on singing his own lyrics to the melody of "Hotel California": *"Welcome to the Museo Re-vo-lu-ci-on. Such a lovely place. Such a lovely place . . ."*

Now whisper in the singer's ear, "Take me to 'Cretin's Corner.'" He'll walk you up the broad staircase. Plead for a detour to peek at Batista's escape passageway—you'll marvel at how bricks and mortar it was compared to your own in the White House. Next, you'll be ushered to the politically incorrect Cretin's Corner. You'll see for yourself the caricatures that heap ridicule on Cuba's most unfavored recent predecessors of yours, Presidents Reagan, Bush, and Bush. A photo of you in front of the caricatures would go hilariously viral—or you could just stick it in your family's private scrapbook. If I don't see it online in the weeks after your visit, I'll know where you're keeping it. No one will know—until my memoirs are published in 2022 or 2023.

street sages

Months after you were elected president almost eight years ago, a man on a Cuban street told me, "Obama will change the US policy toward Cuba. Not in his first term because of American politics, but in his second." One evening last week, an old man in a Camagüey park got me straight on technology. I pointed at two dozen smart phone owners using Wi-Fi, which didn't exist here a year ago. I called it new technology. "It's not new," he corrected me. "Obama sent it to us."

a good night's sleep in Fidel's cabin

If you lack the time on this trip, next year you can explore *La Comandancia* at your leisure and visit Fidel's cabin. It still has the same bed, simply dressed in clean white sheets. No one has slept in it since Fidel in 1958.

I humbly ask that, back in Havana, you make a request for one night's sleep in the cabin—if not for you then for me. I confess to a plan six years in the making to slip into the cabin for a night. I've planned to use the secret trap door in the floor that Fidel built but never used to escape, should adversaries arrive. You wouldn't need to publicize this plum in your trip-concluding communiqué with President Raúl Castro.

hang out at your friends' cabin in Turquino National Park

Just before you make that trip to La Comandancia, whether or not you're planning to overnight in the revolutionary leader's cabin, stop down below in the village of Santo Domingo. Just inside the national park boundary, hidden between the road and the drop-off to the Rio Yara, you'll find Yorbanis's cabin, where he lives with his friend Marbelia. Yorbanis built his humble thatched-roof home from five towering

Yorbanis Viltres strums one of two guitars he owns. He's in a band, too.
Left: Yorbanis Viltres outside the home he built of royal palms on the edge of Santo Domingo, above the River Yara.

royal palms he had permission to harvest. Once cut, he sliced up each tree lengthwise with an axe and metal wedge, then dragged the finely honed boards down mountain trails to build his cabin walls. He traded for nails and electrical wire with vendors passing by on the road. He wondered once if we do the same when building our houses in the United States. I don't know how things work at your place, Mr. President, but I acquire boards, nails, and wire by hoofing it to lumberyards and hardware stores.

Yorbanis will understand if you don't look at him much while conversing. He'll know you're engrossed in what you'll see through the open Brazilian wood shutters: banana, mango, orange and coffee trees, orchids, and all other manner of flowers and plants. Talk to him about Cuban baseball or American politics, or turn to the books about Ernesto "Che" Guevara and Hugo Chavez on the table. If a Bible is there, it belongs to Marbelia.

Walk with Yorbanis through his shaded yard toward the thatched-roof outhouse. You'll see a pestle and mortar—the mortar over 50 years old carved in a slice of tree trunk. He'll pulverize the coffee beans he roasted in the morning over a wood fire a few feet away. You may never again savor a cup of coffee like the cup he'll brew for you in his small and perfectly kept kitchen.

Yorbanis and Marbelia have asked me to invite you and your family to visit them. You can't formally accept the invitation. They have no street address, phone, email, or doorbell; nor do they own a car, bicycle, horse, or mule. Just stroll in.

You might walk 20 minutes with Yorbanis up a road and muddy path to Misael's farmhouse. If Yorbanis is packing a razor blade and two pair of scissors, it's because he'll give Misael a 40-minute outdoor haircut on a calfskin-covered chair. Misael was born near La Comandancia months after the revolution was won. As a young man, he repaired Fidel's cabin and other buildings at the preserved hideout. He farms far-flung tracts of land in a cooperative and is the hardest-working farmer you'll ever meet. He has no television. He has a radio, though. But it broke some time ago.

the boy who watched the attacks get planned

One evening before dark, while in Santo Domingo, cross the River Yara by footbridge or hop from boulder to boulder to Juan and Maria Castillo's house.

In his grandfather Lucas's house, Juan had a ringside seat as the townsfolk were won over by Fidel Castro and Che Guevara and their band of guerillas, all hunted with a vengeance by Dictator Batista. Juan was eight years old when the rebels slipped quietly into his home. He watched as those congregated, including Lucas, made battle plans. You might wonder aloud if Fidel ever slept in the house. Juan will tell you that one evening, his grandparents tidied up the best bedroom. Fidel Castro stayed for the night.

Juan, an eyewitness *extraordinaire* with an incredible memory of the revolution, would be pleased to have you in for a campesino supper on a mountain-built table in their dirt floor kitchen. It's eye-popping to contemplate the questions you might ask, especially since you've read 2,900 President's Daily Briefs that reveal some of the most sensitive and surprising top-secret intelligence in recent world history.

When you leave Juan and Maria's house in the deep darkness of night, you'll have in hand a bag of coffee from the very farm that fed the revolutionaries. It is the land that keeps on giving.

Please don't think that a flashlight will help you find your way down to the river, unless you have all night and you're not one to panic as your batteries wear down. Just ask Juan to show you the way. He's been walking this trail since he was a young child.

Mr. President, if you're engrossed in other causes and can't make it to the Sierra Maestra in the next couple of years, I resolve as follows:

I will personally interview and film Juan Castillo, produce a history-gripping microdocumentary, and personally report to you—and to the wider public on my website, TomsGlobe.com.

Humbly at your service,

Advance Man

Santo Domingo ballplayers take a break on their ballfield—the road that leads steeply up the mountains to Fidel Castro's revolution-era secret command post, La Comandancia.

CANADA

Total Strangers
AUGUST 18–SEPTEMBER 2, 2014

For some time, I'll be thinking about the total strangers I met by
accident in Canada:

meet the Hutterites

"Do you have a couple liters of gas I could buy?" I ask the three blond
boys after riding my motorcycle up their farm driveway in seemingly
gas station–free Manitoba. I'd forgotten to gas up in Warroad before
I crossed over from Minnesota. These were the very first hours of my
trip across the woods, prairie, and mountain provinces, and I was sure
I'd be lucky.

"No. We only have diesel," the oldest boy informs me. But he then
explains in his distinct, non-Canadian accent how I can find gas at a
one-pump town on a side road. I want to inquire where his accent
came from, but I'm now in a foreign country where everyone is a total
stranger. I won't pry for personal information. Perhaps everyone in
his family has the same accent—all 16 of them, a fact I did learn. In
Winnipeg, a café waiter later ventures that they must be Hutterites,
the descendants of a closely knit religious community who left Germany
for North America in the 1870s. I wonder for how many more generations they will keep their accent.

why not ride the ancient horse?

Polar bears abound at the Winnipeg Zoo and are the big reason for going there. Unless it's a warm day, in which case you won't see any. Instead, watch ancient horses from Asia, the last remaining wild breed, called "Przewalski's horse." Inform a young schoolgirl this horse was once considered extinct, except for a few living in zoos. "They're wild," you tell the girl.

"Does that mean you can't ride?" she asks.

"Right."

"And if you do," she wisely posits, "you'll fall off and break . . . break . . ."

"Break what?" I want to know.

"Break everything on you."

Neither of us climbs over the fence to try.

walking Gravelbourg with a future pediatric orthodontic surgeon

If you're like some people, you'll travel out of your way to see Gravelbourg, a French-speaking town on the Saskatchewan prairie with its famous church. Grade-12 Sara might be your guide, and you can't help thinking she's just told you the most fascinating story ever on a town's origin. She explains that in 1906, the first French Prime Minister of Canada, a Liberal, wanted to populate Canada's distant prairies with French Canadians who'd be advocates for the Liberal Party. He enticed the large Gravel family to found a distant town.

To this day, 70% of Gravelbourg's residents speak at least some French, and Sara attends a school where every class is taught in French. The huge church—the province's first cathedral—took just a year to build, Sara explains, but the priest-artist spent 10 years painting incredible Bible scenes inside. He painted them on the back of linoleum, a material cheaper than canvas yet quite durable.

"What career will you pursue, Sara?" I wonder.

"I want to be a pediatric orthodontic surgeon. I'll go to the University of Saskatchewan in Saskatoon."

"What do you and your friends do around here for fun?" I wonder a little more.

"On a Sunday, we might travel to Waterton Lakes National Park, just north of the USA's Glacier Park. Or, like last night, we saw the movie *Let's Be Cops*. It's silly but funny."

I ask the grade-11 gas station attendant the same question. He and his buddies might drive 70 miles to Moose Jaw "and hang out in McDonald's," he answers. That sounds silly and funny: why don't they walk to Gravelbourg's Main Street and see *Let's Be Cops* or *Boyhood?*

don't gulp on the dinosaur angle

A couple at a diner in Swift Current, Saskatchewan, tells me they are heading to the rural town of Eastend. Since I am knowledgeable—having read a newspaper—I advise them not to get crunched by a T. rex. (The world's most complete T. rex skeleton was found in Eastend.) The man says they are going to his aunt's 90th birthday party, "a dinosaur herself." *GULP!* he almost hears me choke out, but I feel he must be joking.

don't miss the best in the west

A French family and I hop in a gondola to ride up the mountain from the town of Banff. With us are other world travelers, as well as locals from nearby Calgary and Edmonton, and from provinces ranging from British Columbia on the Pacific to the Atlantic. Many are Asian-Canadians. Others are First Nation families from Canada, perhaps the Mikisew Cree, Sunchild, or Athabasca Chipewyan.

The family from Paris has visited Seattle, British Columbia, and Banff (which, with three adjoining parks, must be the most beautiful national park complex in the world). I ask the family what place was their favorite, and most surprising—surely I'd hear "Banff" blurted out in family unison. But the high school son (who loves his physics classes) pipes up, "The Boeing Factory near Seattle." His mom points to the Boeing cap he bought during the factory tour. Later at the Lake Louise hostel, two German college students tell me they are heading to that factory too. My motorcycle trip west stops 515 miles short of Boeing. I might have to fly there someday.

stick it in your gas tank

I pull over in Kootenay National Park, on the Continental Divide a few feet inside British Colombia from Alberta. My motorcycle's gas gauge registers 3/4 full, but I don't trust it. When you're chilled and low on oxygen, your mind starts to disbelieve your instruments and instructs your hands to take over. With great effort, I break a branch off a resistant bush and stick it down my gas tank to see how much gets soaked. Aha! I have only a gallon of gas left, like I guessed. I cut my Kootenay tour short and return to the town of Banff.

As I gas up, the visiting tour bus driver pumping $700 in his tank wants me to see all his scars "from falling off a motorbike in Thailand last year." I explain how I ripped off a branch in Kootenay and found out I was down to a gallon of gas. He retorts that people go to jail for destroying trees in Canada's national parks.

Besides, he says, the Canadian branch I used measures in liters. Not gallons.

the four-year-old knows where it is

As I hike a trail in Sunshine Meadows, which runs up and over the Continental Divide in Banff National Park, I see a "spruce island" moving across the nearly treeless meadow. Or do I? I can vouch only for this: Some time ago, seeds released from opening spruce cones blew or were perhaps carried by birds up to this nearly treeless elevation. Two or three seeds landed in a sweet spot, germinated, and grew. But within a few short years, the bitter wind degraded the spruce branches on the trees' windswept side, imperiling the trees. As luck had it, the trees' seeds that embedded themselves in the ground on the leeward side took root and grew robustly. The process of death on the windswept side of the spruce island and new tree life on the protected side has continued over decades. The island appears (to the most imaginative eye) to creep across the meadow. Keep your eyes open during your walk in Sunshine Meadows—you'll see several more islands, some only about the size of a living room. Remember they're all moving, each likely at its own pace.

I came to Sunshine Meadows because a woman at my bed and breakfast told me it's the "most beautiful place ever in the whole entire world." I'm not going to quibble. (She also said her mother describes Lake Moraine, not far away, as a glacier-fed lake reflecting ten mountain peaks that is "so beautiful it'll make you cry." It was so cloudy it made me grumble.)

If you visit the "most beautiful place ever in the whole entire world" looking for the spruce islands or another alpine phenomenon, ask a four-year-old hiker for directions. You'll recognize him, for he sits on a stone at a fork in the trail studying maps (while his parents wait). He'll tell you where you're at and where he has been. "Tell me," you might say, "why do you love maps so much?" He'll answer—without even looking up—"Because you can tell where it is." A day may come, I fret, when every four-year-old will learn that real maps have gone the way of the dinosaur.

why not just bike for seven years (around the world)

At Lake Louise, hostel guest Fumi from Japan tells me he's been traveling for a year and a half. After exclaiming "wow!" I ask his new acquaintance Ryo ("Rio") how long *he's* been traveling. "Five years. I have two more to go," Ryo says. Fumi informs me that Ryo is bicycling around the world in seven years and is famous in Japan. Ryo has two more dreams, he tells me: open a café-museum in his hometown of Nagano, and bicycle to the moon. Let's keep an eye on him, I tell myself.

Later, when I search "ryohei oguchi bicycle," I feel bad I didn't offer to buy him a meal—he'd been scraping by and sleeping outdoors nearly everywhere, like Australia, Vietnam, Cambodia, Tibet, and France. He'll be hitting 100 countries, I read. Don't we all believe in Ryohei! He would actually visit 157 countries in nine years, posting incredible photos on Instagram.

go Greyhound to tundra

You may be visiting the Greyhound station, perhaps the one in Banff's old railroad depot, if you're like me and forget a camera in the Econo Lodge back in Lethbridge. Or if you leave your phone charger, wallet, iPad, shoes, or sweatshirt in Regina, Swift Current, Medicine Hat, or Moose Jaw, as the agent says we tourists are wont to do. Your motel will speed it to you on the next Greyhound. Since the agent has a free minute, ask her something far out like, "What is the most exotic destination Greyhound travels to in Canada?"

"If you want exotic," she'll tell you, "book a trip to the tundra of the Yukon or Northwest Territories. In the summer." And before the permafrost disappears forever, I say to myself.

what about the radium in Radium Hot Springs?

If you do manage to put enough liters of gas in your tank, cross the Continental Divide on Highway 93 and descend the Rockies into Radium Hot Springs, British Columbia. Reward yourself by slipping into one of the hot pools. If you ask the lifeguard taking samples of the water whether she's "checking the radium," she'll reassure you that the pools are healthy and heavenly every day.

Head-Smashed-In
SEPTEMBER 1, 3450 B.C.

It was a fine autumn day on September 1, 3450 B.C. The world's first wheel was now about 100 years old. The Mesopotamian inventors had not affixed it to a chariot yet, being content to let potters make use of it. *Tom! Tap your head; this is not about Mesopotamia!* On that autumn day, my patrilineal ancestor was preparing for a harsh winter in today's Russia. His descendants were still one or two thousand years shy of arriving in Finland. According to a 2010 DNA analysis, the lineage already had 60,000 years of travel under its belt—*Tom, slap your head; this is not about you. You and your ancestors have no role in this story!*[2]

Tens of millions of buffalo roamed North America's Great Plains on that fine autumn day. Hundreds pastured on a minor Rocky Mountain slope 70 miles south of present-day Calgary in Alberta. Before sundown on that date in 3450 B.C., most of that herd would be dead and partly butchered up for winter subsistence by a native tribe building on their grandparents' bright idea.

Weeks of observation, debate, and preparations preceded that Big Event of September 1. (That's the date in my mind, and the year is likely right too, since this event probably took place almost every year, starting about a century earlier.) The unsuspecting buffalo were about to be channeled, lured, and stampeded straight over a cliff. The bright idea didn't work exactly as planned, though, since some turned right before the unseen drop-off, fortuitously escaping the smashing fate of the other buffalo (now more properly called "bison," some say).

why did they pick an autumn day for the stampede? In summer and fall, the grasses on the slope were high in protein. The buffalo meat was also rich in fat after months of good grazing. The hides were covered with long, thick hair against the coming cold.

---

[2] See "A Brief History of Traveling Genes" later in this book for my ancestors' full itinerary.

The herds of cows and calves were calmer, since the males went off on their own after mating. The onset of cool weather helped retard spoilage of the carcasses. What a perfect time to execute a communal buffalo hunt!

Over the 5,465 years after 3450 B.C., more happened:

why was the jump once abandoned
for over 1,000 years?

Weigh in with your theory; others have. The grasslands and animals may have been affected by environmental changes, reducing the number of buffalo. New people unfamiliar with complex hunting techniques may have arrived. Perhaps, and certainly intriguing to all of us . . . [space reserved for *your* theories]. In any case, stampedes revved up again after the hiatus and continued from 200 A.D. to 1850. After that, rampant gunfire reduced the North American population from 60 million animals to just hundreds.

why were many of the bone layers burned?

Archaeological excavations at the bottom of the cliff have revealed layers of heavily burned bone. The hunting community may have fired the bones and debris to clean up the landing pad for future kills. Otherwise, the smell of rotting carcasses might have frightened off the coming herds. This practice would also have kept away scavengers such as wolves, coyotes, and grizzly bears. Another possibility is that natural prairie fires swept through, igniting the grease, hair, and bones left behind at the kill.

My hunch is that the hunters didn't want the jump to be rendered unusable by the buildup of bones. Even with all the burning, the bottom of the cliff is only about half as far down as it once was. Or one might hypothesize that burning was a proper burial practice, since many native peoples honored the buffalo and considered them a spirit that influenced their lives.

what caused 4,000 or more herds to stampede over
the cliff since 3600 B.C.?

Chasing the buffalo on horseback, I would think, right? *Wrong!*
Native Americans did not possess horses until far more recently. So
swift runners chased precipitously gathered herds on foot, I'd conclude.
*What? This know-it-all supposition is a wanton oversimplification,
Tom! Do you need your head smacked in? If you want to elbow in on
this story, first educate yourself. The buffalo jump's interpretive centre
might be a wise place for you to start.*

All right, then. Know your prey. Buffalo have a keen sense of smell
but poor vision. Cows are wary of predators and protective of calves.
The camp sent out young men as buffalo runners to lure grazing buffalo
into the drive lanes. Some runners disguised themselves under buffalo
calf skins, others under wolf skins. Those disguised as calves bellowed
calf cries from the direction of the cliff. Those disguised as wolves
stalked the herd, nudging it slowly forward. This whole time, the
buffalo talked to each other with grunts and signaled with their tails,
but to no lasting avail.

After these runners had labored for days, the herd was set up for
a surprise in the drive lane. Many men and women were hidden along
both sides of the lane, one each in a cairn of stones, branches, and debris.
They stepped out from behind the cairns and urged the herd steadily
toward the jump and away from gaps in the drive lanes.

Near the cliff, hunters leapt out from behind their cairns where
they'd been hiding, panicking the herd into a densely packed stampede
toward the cliff. The runners who'd been stalking the animals for miles
could finally rest—as long as they escaped stray buffalo that might
trample them.

did the buffalo meat get all rotten
in the autumn sunshine?

Not all community members were involved in stampeding the buffalo.
Many had been busy for days at the bottom of the cliff. By the time

the first buffalo crashed, pots of water were steaming, stones were well heated to boil fat and marrow, knives and scrapers were at the ready, and meat drying racks were erected.

The people at the bottom speared any buffalo that survived the fall, skinned all the deceased, butchered them, cut the meat in thin strips, and hung the strips to dry. Later, they beat the strips into shreds, poured melted buffalo tallow into the pounded meat, added berries or dried fruit, and stirred. They packed the mixture into buffalo skin bags. It cooled and hardened and lasted a year. They ate it dry or boiled it in water. The surplus of this nutritious pemmican was used in trade.

did the buffalo of 3450 B.C. hold the record for being mammoth-sized game animals?

An early buffalo species was twice as big as the species that lived in 3450 B.C . We know the earlier behemoths were sometimes approached and killed in marshy spots—next to a creek in Northern Minnesota, for example. Perhaps Mario, a Mayan friend of mine in Guatemala, had ancestors who participated in these North American kills. After all, his DNA analysis last year showed he has distant cousins (relatively speaking) among today's Ojibwe, Sioux, and Cherokee people.[3]

While the early buffalo species was huge, the record for mammoth size among North American game animals probably belongs to a member of the elephant family. It's known as the woolly mammoth. It stood 11 feet high, weighed tons, and ran 25 to 35 mph. The Clovis hunters stacked mammoth carcasses in piles in present-day Wyoming and let them freeze solid, returning when they needed meat. By 11,000 B.C. or even earlier, it had been hunted to extinction in mainland North America. The mammoth did, however, survive on Saint Paul Island off the Alaska coast until 3600 B.C., when they likely died due to the

---

[3] See "Ancestral Walks," deployed with other Guatemalan adventures a little later.

increasing scarcity of fresh water to drink, which is essential for these behemoths to avoid overheating.[4]

what's the name of the Canadian buffalo jump, for crying out loud?

One day, perhaps a few centuries ago in September, a curious boy had an inventive idea. He wanted to see the stampeding buffalo fall in front of his very eyes. He crouched against the cliff, near the bottom. The trouble was, a lot of buffalo were falling in front of his eyes. The dead and wounded piled up and crushed him. Hence, the name Head-Smashed-In Buffalo Jump.

P.S. Never watch a buffalo jump from a precarious position. One may get an idea from the safety of home by searching "unesco.org buffalo jump."

[4] Russell Graham et al., "Timing and causes of mid-Holocene mammoth extinction on Saint Paul Island, Alaska," Proceedings of the National Academy of Sciences of the United States of America 113, no. 33 (August 16, 2016) (pnas.org).

THE UNITED STATES

A Strange Warning about an American Town
SEPTEMBER 6, 2014

"Don't visit Browning," the stranger in Glacier National Park from Great Falls, Montana, obliquely warns me.

"But that town does have a museum," I point out.

Her second terse warning leaves words unsaid, like the first—what words, I just don't know. She is only willing to imply that Browning, 40 miles east of Glacier on US Hwy. 2, is a sketchy, even dangerous place.

That very day, I hang around Browning for several unexpected hours.

The Conoco gas station is the community focal point on Friday at 5 p.m. I pay for gas and the coffee I need to stay awake for 60 more miles. Outside, I set the coffee on a vending machine and move my motorcycle away from the pump in respect of the idling pickup waiting to advance. Once the pickup gasses up, four boys jump out of the tinted-window crew cab and push the truck. That's how the driver gets it started. Few customers fill up, buying just $5 or $10 worth. Finished with the coffee, I go back inside to observe town life. After waiting in line, I pay for a huckleberry-flavored ice cream bar and two newspapers to learn later on what is happening.

The Conoco cashier drives 40 miles to work and to attend the community college. Most everyone in town, it seems, has energy, a mission, a smile, and a talkative manner. Now again, it's time to leave town. "First, though," I tell myself, "I'll ride the few streets in town, north and south, east and west." That throws my schedule for a loop, for I smell *football in the air*. The first game of the season pits the Whitefish Bulldogs against the Browning Indians. My hand is stamped at the ticket booth for $5. The scoreboard counts down the 46 minutes to kickoff. The food stand volunteers take time and care in preparing my fully loaded burrito, which they promise I'll love. The stands are full of local fans. A handful of the Bulldogs' parents have made the 93-mile drive from the other side of Glacier National Park.

I sit in the middle of 200 Browning townsfolk, pulling for the hometown team, of course. The metal benches vibrate sharply as kids run up and down, looking for family, friends, and fun.

Tonight, the visiting Bulldogs, from larger and upscale Whitefish, are just too powerful. Yet the local fans never lose their passion and recognition that this is just a game. They give a warm applause to an injured Whitefish Bulldog when he finally rises and limps off the field.

It's halftime, it's sunset, and it's chilling off fast. I need to ride to Shelby at 65 mph over the Northern Great Plains since I've made a motel reservation. Leaving the game, I ask the ticket agent to stamp my program just like she stamped my hand. "I'll take this home to Minnesota." She points at her colored-purple hair—it's the Browning team color. "Just like my Minnesota Vikings," I say. I've spent hours in Browning. The museum was worth speeding down Glacier's mountains to get to in time. Conoco was a blast. The streets were vibrant. The game was a hoot.

I finally ride off at 8 p.m., the Browning cheerleaders' cheer bouncing around in my head (a cheer familiar to some older Americans, just with their own team's name inserted):

Everywhere we go-ohh, everywhere we go-ohh,
People want to know-ohh, people want to know-ohh,

Whoo we are, whoo we are,

Sohh we tell them, sohh we tell them,

We are the Indians, the mighty mighty Indians,

We are (repeat!).

This was "sketchy" Browning. These are its people—Conoco employees and customers, museum workers, football fans, and volunteers. And cheerleaders like Shawntyana Bullshoe and Shaylee Devereau. And football players with last names like Red Horn (5'8"), Heavyrunner (6'3"), Little Plume (5'6"), Old Chief (6'1"), Kicking Woman (6'2"), and Arrowtopknot (6'3").

Blackfeet all, dedicated to the game, embracing each other and the future.

As I ride my motorcycle away, Glacier's glistening mountain peaks fade into the sunset in both rearview mirrors. The only warning about Browning that I can trust is a road sign just out of town, cautioning of high winds. Since a transplanted airport wind sock hangs from the top of the road sign post, you can see for yourself. Pushed by the wind, a red fox speeds across the highway just in front of me. *BEWARE!* if you visit Browning, on Montana's Blackfeet Indian Reservation.

traveler's postscript:

My brain was showered with facts of life at the Museum of the Plains Indian, thanks to the work of hundreds of Native Americans from the mid-1800s (crafts and artifacts of 11 Northern Plains tribal peoples) right down to today (museum staff). The rich arts on display are of the Blackfeet, Crow, Northern Cheyenne, Sioux, Assiniboine, Arapaho, Shoshone, Nez Perce, Flathead, Chippewa, and Cree.

Before visiting the museum, I might have speculated in two sentences what I knew about the Indians' use of horses. But now . . .

Southern Plains Indians first acquired horses in the 1600s from the Spanish, who bred them near Santa Fe. During the 1700s, horses were traded farther and farther north, even to present-day Canada. Horses were valuable in hunting and warfare, in the search for food, and in pursuit of a safer or better place to live. Earlier, only dogs and humans pulled the cargo travois—two poles trailing behind, bearing a cargo platform or net. Horses could pull heavier travois loads when a band or tribe made its frequent moves.

Stealing horses from enemy villages was a widely recognized feat of bravery. Bravery—more than killing—was stressed in warfare. Weapons were developed or modified for more effective use by horse-back riders. The lifestyle change from foot to horseback, I've read, was one of the quickest and most successful in human history.

Native Americans spent months on dozens of tasks preparing for winter, the museum explains. One example: Buffalo hides, tanned and painted, were hung inside the tepee's buffalo hide walls to better insulate the interior. When moving to a new location, tepees and all the parts were hauled on the travois.

Before the horse, many a Blackfeet must have walked the distance of twice around the earth in their lifetimes on scouting, hunting, food gathering, trading, recreational, religious, defensive and offensive, and moving missions (my own calculations presented). Some of these people, when elderly, may have been moved by horse-pulled travois to a new seasonal settlement, having taken some 110 million steps in their lifetimes.

What personal stories they must have been remembering and sharing! Some of those experiences and incidents might have happened quickly, in just ten steps; others in a million steps.

If you're near Glacier, be sure to pay a visit to Browning and its museum, football season or not. I talked to a Minnesota friend yesterday who'd done just that last year. He agrees that you'll find it rewarding.

AROUND THE WORLD IN 400 DAYS

AROUND THE WORLD IN 400 DAYS

As the American and Canadian West of 2014 disappeared in the sunset behind my motorcycle, I imagined that I was once again cheering the Browning Indians under the Big Sky of Montana, poking around the Alberta buffalo jump that victimized about four thousand stampeded herds since 3500 B.C., and soaking up Radium Hot Springs in British Columbia. As more miles rolled by—my helmeted head, booted feet, gloved hands, and leathered torso protected from an array of dangers and discomforts—I imagined how different life would be if my hands never touched handlebars or steering wheels.

Just then, my mind recalled that, in a not-so-bygone era, I had not touched a handlebar or steering wheel for 15 straight months. I'd embarked on a tour of the Western and Eastern Hemispheres. The excursion ranged from 88 miles north of the equator to the Arctic Circle, covered 36,000 miles, and took me to 26 countries (if I count a hurried 30-second sojourn to North Korea). My absolutely favorite two or three countries? Oh, that's too tough to answer. Let's see what might have been *your* favorite experiences.

Minneapolis to liftoff from LA

My red Volkswagen Bug, well built in West Germany in 1964, was reluctant to climb the Rockies out of Denver in June '70, though it had cruised smoothly all the way from Minneapolis. Checking with a mechanic, it needed a ring and valve job. Figuring the bill would be less in Boulder, I headed north to that University of Colorado city. A two-day stay in a frat house was free since I was willing to do janitorial. A carpenter then invited me deep into the mountains where he was building a cabin. The night sky repeatedly broke loose with thunder and lightning. He darted out of the tent to watch, insisting I follow him every time.

The Bug repair completed, I climbed the Rockies and drove all the way to Los Angeles. I spent time in a University of Southern California frat house—free because I once again did janitorial—and hung out in the Los Angeles Coliseum during USC football games— free because I was an usher. In Manhattan Beach (or was it Redondo Beach?), I made a summer friend sitting on the next bar stool. He looked to me like he could be a brother Elvis never knew. A couple of nights at 2 a.m. (or was it 5 a.m.?), we drove down Santa Monica Boulevard from central LA all the way to the Pacific Ocean. The sun would soon rise on that end of Route 66, the original course from Chicago through St. Louis, Tulsa, Amarillo, Tucumcari, Winslow, and Barstow already well-illuminated by that rising star I'd soon be chasing westerly for 15 months.

the otherworldly Western Pacific

Come late August, a jet lifted off from Los Angeles, carrying my Minnesota friend Tom Woxland and me on an adventure we'd planned months earlier. Our tickets listed destinations from Honolulu to New Delhi. Seeing Hawaii, I realized I could live there for a lifetime. But we soon zipped through five more time zones—and found ourselves confounded by how to put food into our mouths. Studying the technique of five women at the next table, we began to use chopsticks.

One day, with the emperor's palace in view, we asked others if that was where Hirohito lived. They didn't seem to understand. Did we mispronounce Hirohito's name, or did his subjects call him by an honorific title? I'm not sure. He's now referred to by his post-humous name, Emperor Shōwa. He'd become the 124th emperor of Japan in 1926 and would reign until 1989.

A train ride away from Tokyo, we experienced the Osaka World's Fair. Standing in line four hours to see the fair's most popular exhibit, I made a few entries in a secretarial notebook I'd found with shorthand symbols printed on the cover. The young person behind me stared quizzically at the symbols, probably trying to figure out what language it was that I wrote and spoke. We didn't speak each other's language, for sure.

Japanese youth hostels, just dollars a day and set in the most beautiful environs of each city, were every young foreign and domestic traveler's choice. One evening, a German backpacker and I resolved to experience a Japanese tradition dating from the 14th-century, the Noh Theater. We discovered dance, music, drama, costumes, and masks that told a tale from traditional Japanese literature. Afterward, we celebrated his birthday with drinks among bright lights.

Upon our return, the hostel was dark and locked up tight. We contemplated climbing a tree, squirreling along a limb, and squeezing into a second-floor window. We decided, instead, to walk along the rain-soaked side of the hostel, climb through the window of a spic-and-span clean communal bath, deposit our shoes with 40 other pairs inside the main door, and have a restful sleep, dreaming about the 14th century. Putting on our shoes to go out the next day, the young man in charge made a beeline for us. Pointing to our shoes' dried mud, he mentioned we'd left tracks all the way from the open window to the shoe rack, termed the transgression a "bad act," and evicted us. On to a different hostel it was.

The days remaining in Japan were now numbered in single digits, but eventfully, a University of Kanazawa student conversed with Tom Woxland and me at that second hostel. Our new friend Kimpei urged

---

[5] Mrs. Matsuda's long life is noted in the part "Asia: 2006 and 2010."

us to visit him in Kanazawa, a seaside city facing the Koreas. A week later, Kimpei greeted us at the Kanazawa train station, one of the world's most beautiful. For a week, we all slept a ladder climb up in a family home's miniscule tatami-matted rental room. Then Kimpei's professor told us about a large room in an old samurai house owned by Mr. and Mrs. Matsuda. It was free because the Matsudas were intrigued by travelers from distant lands and were generous people.[5] Our continued survival now meant teaching English to an assortment of students just three hours a week. My traveling companion Tom and I ate lunch at the university cafeteria every day for 100 yen—just thirty cents. We'd find Japanese meals and Chinese gyoza in hole-in-the-wall cafés with space for six or seven patrons.

Kimpei introduced Tom and me to members of the university's English Speaking Society. Some students had never talked to an American before. By then, our initial two-week plan for Japan was being wildly overshot, which was enough time for one of us to assume a slightly different identity. Students renamed Tom as Blue (or Blue-san) to distinguish him from me and because he traveled with an ultralight wardrobe of blue clothes. I remained Tom—or Tom-san, Mr. Tom, or Tomu.

Most every street in the old part of Kanazawa led us to a surprising dead end or to a turn at angles we called obtuse, acute, or reflex in high school geometry. Was this the result of "ad hoc city planning?" No. The samurai "city fathers" so designed the grid centuries ago to confound and trap invaders. Now, visitors are eager to explore these Kanazawa streets, the castle on the university grounds, and, in every season, the expansive Kenroku-en Park, one of the "Three Great Gardens" of Japan.

Months later, Tom decided to search for an Australian-bound ocean freighter to jump on. I stayed back and spent a total of eight months in Japan, enjoying Kanazawa's heavy snow from the Sea of Japan, followed by feverish melts never seen in Minnesota until spring.

I played the role of "Doctor" in *Sin and Crime,* an English-language play written by a student. The playwright cast himself as Jesus, Kimpei as a lawyer, and others as a prison inmate and a ghost. One weekend, I journeyed by train to a snowy mountain retreat with members of the English Speaking Society. Cold it was, although we slept on a tatami-matted floor like spokes extending from the hub of a wheel, our feet under a coffee table–like electric heater, with quilts layered all the way to our chins.

South Korea and North Korea would be the next two destinations —a side trip by boat from Japan. My first South Korean meal was with people at a restaurant table next to mine, since they saw me eating alone. They grilled tender beef bulkogi on hot coals in the middle of our table. When they learned my heritage was Finnish, one exclaimed, "You are my cousin!" He believed Finns and Koreans to be related. Panmunjom, on the border with North Korea, was a spot within grasp. A group I joined visited the negotiating hall whose northern half is in North Korea, with the border running down the middle of the long confer-ence table. Circling the table, we scurried in and out of North Korea.

Back in Japan, I explored Nagasaki and then Hiroshima, sitting behind a man on a bus whose neck had suffered severe burns some-time earlier—I believe at exactly 8:16 a.m. on August 6, 1945, when the atomic bomb let loose from the Enola Gay detonated.

I weaved my way through a small Hiroshima parking lot and found the bomb's hypocenter—the spot directly below the aerial detonation point. Years later, I'd also stand at the spot where the bomb was loaded onto the Enola Gay on Tinian Island, 1,570 miles southeast of Hiroshima, and I'd tramp old grounds in Los Alamos, New Mexico, where the hypersecret atomic bomb was developed.

Needing to make up time through an ocean of Japan's rice paddies and over the mountains, I did what some said was unheard of: sticking a thumb out to hitch a ride. Three young people soon picked me up. After awhile, they seemed about to invite me to drive. But before I could put my foot down, one overruled the others. He said, I think, that I didn't have a clue how to drive on the left side of the highway, or in a car with the steering wheel on the right.

This is how, for 15 months, my hands did not touch a steering wheel or handlebars.

After two months in Tokyo's Shibuya District—teaching English, working as a waiter till 2 a.m. in a Shinjuku night club, and studying Japanese—I headed to Taiwan, which was next on the air ticket I'd purchased so long before. On a bus to Hualien from the capital of Taipei, a young couple realized I could say a few things in Japanese, having used reel-to-reel tapes Kimpei recorded for me. Bits of the Japanese language had been passed down to them from their parents' World War II generation. We communicated using a dozen sentences. They were Taipei residents traveling to their hometown to celebrate a family wedding.

Before we'd traveled a couple more kilometers, I was invited to the wedding. We stayed in a parent's house for two days for the half-Westernized wedding and feast. What a treat the wedding party was for a North American fresh out of college and already dazed by the world. The Taipei couple and I returned to the capital after the festive days, and they invited me to bed down on their apartment's kitchen floor. In later years, I attempted to contact them, hoping to mail them a full-color (but silent) 8 mm film I had shot of the wedding. I didn't succeed.

I'm still pained that they, the wedding couple, and their children (and grandchildren) will never see the movie I've safely kept. And how could I ever find Ko Zung Keng and his wife now? I suppose I could start by zeroing in on the Amis indigenous population and the Amis name of the large family: Tsu Gao Dango. The Amis, one of sixteen Austronesian cultures in Taiwan, is the island's largest group of urban aborigines.

Consulting my plane ticket, I realized Hong Kong was my next destination. By 1971, the harbor plied by hundreds of traditional

Chinese junks had changed little in centuries—at least according to how the harbor of the 1840s was depicted in the epic novel *Tai-Pan* by James Clavell. This makes me think that 1971 was closer in time to the 1840s than it was to 2006, when I next visited Hong Kong.

A hint of change in 1971 was a new-fangled mode of transportation: a hydrofoil that skimmed over the water to and from Macau, a Portuguese colony on "Mainland Red China." Since I'd stepped into North Korea briefly, I thought I might tiptoe into China from Macau for a few seconds, perhaps decades or generations before tourists would be allowed. At the border with Red China, it was obvious that, though the Chinese guards would let me get to within ten feet, any further advance would be met with—well, I didn't push my luck.

the troubled Southeast Asia

War-torn Vietnam was now only 935 miles to the south. The few of us foreign travelers were mostly young backpackers who congregated in downtown Saigon, deciding which restaurant to try out or which bar to frequent. Vietnamese travel destinations were few during the war, though I learned I could hop on a boat to cross the Saigon River and visit a rural settlement on the other side. Over there, just before a heavy rain, young boys ran around pointing at me, saying, "He Viet Cong, he Viet Cong." I stood outside under the rickety roof of a small store, waiting for the storm to pass and for a boat back to Saigon. Hearing the next day that I could hop aboard a United States Army bus heading to the sprawling military base of Long Binh, I went. Stepping off that bus, one could wander around freely among the soldiers who were fast becoming veterans of a foreign war.

Back in Saigon, I aimed to fly to Vientienne, Laos, but the only other passenger and I were told that the flight had been cancelled that week. With only two passengers flying from one capital to another, we figured it was not economical—and might not be economical the following week either. I thus flew south toward the equator to Singapore and

Malaysia, back north to Cambodia's capital Phnom Penh, and on to Thailand and Burma.

the unreachable highlight of Cambodia

A major reason travelers have visited Cambodia since the 12th century has been to see and succumb to the Angkor Hindu temples scattered over many miles. Moreover, a stone carving 2,000 feet in length portrays Hindu epics, crucial battles, and mythological spirits. Alas, Cambodia's war footing in 1971 foreclosed travel to the town of Siem Reap and the Angkor ruins. Thus, perhaps the most stupendous architectural experience in the world was off-limits. My experiences as I was confined in the capital of Phnom Penh in 1971 (such as being frightened off a barbed-wire barricade by a gunshot) are closely related to experiences during a trip in 2017—and the focus of a writing still in development. (Check for developments on TomsGlobe.com.)

the disdainful water buffalo I drove to distraction

Heading north on a bus from Bangkok toward Chiangmai, I sensed someone looking over my shoulder from the seat behind, about to speak. As I climbed down from the bus with my backpack, finding a place to stay at this destination was not my task. Instead, I joined my new friend on a small bus leaving town toward a rural agricultural college where he was a student.

I slept on the wood floor of a farmhouse porch with my friend. "Thai people are more afraid of mosquitoes than tigers," he told me as we turned in for the night. We then made sure there weren't any gaps in the mosquito net enveloping us. We were thus safe from the greater of two threats.

The next morning, he treated me to a once-in-a-lifetime experience. Across the road, he and a neighbor farmer suggested that I take my hand at plowing the field. I could do that, I thought, since as a teenager I created a garden in my Biwabik, Minnesota, backyard in the rock- and clay-filled ground a few hundred feet from an iron mine pit. And the soil here in Northern Thailand was beautiful! Not so beautiful—but menacing!—was the "tool" I'd use to plow this fertile soil: a huge water buffalo.

"Just hold on to the plow behind the water buffalo and you will both move forward," my friend explained. And hold on for dear life I did, for the animal, unimpressed with its new master, began running. I feared it was working toward a gallop! I also feared that if my hands let go of the plow, the valuable water buffalo would not stop moving until it got into the mountains. And then, how would the farmer plow his field? But I soon had no choice, for I couldn't keep this up. I let go of the plow. Thankfully, the water buffalo stopped. It turned its head and gave me the most disdainful look of its life, a look I can see to this day.

martial law and *Newsweek*

The incredible country of Burma (now Myanmar) had been ruled under martial law ever since a 1962 coup d'état removed the civilian leadership under Prime Minister U Nu. I found my personal headquarters in a family hotel in Pagan (now Bagan). The 2,000 Buddhist temples within a few miles of Pagan rival the ancient ruins of Cambodia's Angkor Wat and Peru's Machu Picchu. I would visit dozens of temples over days.

My source of news on this world trip was the weekly newsmagazine *Newsweek*. I faithfully read every word, save a sentence here and there. Once I finished with an issue, I wouldn't even think of dumping it in the trash. The issue I took with me to Burma critiqued the military dictatorship in that country. "What will I do with this issue now that I've read every article in it?" I asked myself. Surely not leave it on a park bench, in a temple, or even in my room, I knew, for it might be traced to me. After three days of getting to know the hotel owner, I felt we could trust each other. I offered the *Newsweek* to him, gently pointing out the article on Burma (that the dictatorship would strongly disapprove of). He accepted my offer. Once he finished reading the magazine, did he pass it to a trusted friend or burn it? I cannot say, but I've wondered ever since.

a million miles away

From Burma's sea-level airport, the jet carried me hours northwest and to a much higher altitude.

I wasn't supposed to be here on my own, not in these mountains, a million miles from anywhere. I was, at least, given a quickly scribbled dictionary with two phrases: *Jonnie bato kaha*—? ("Is this the path to—?") and the phrase for "Do you have food?" The question whether someone "has food" also implicitly meant, "And I'll sleep here." If a home serves a traveler an evening meal, he or she may sleep on the floor (for free). Before starting out, I was also handed a bare-bones hand-drawn map showing a line jiggling to the left and right with a couple of village names inserted. One darkened area over the line portrayed a rain forest and silently warned that, before entering, I had to find someone to guide me through. After a couple of days, once I got to the end of the line on the map, I was to turn around and seek my way back.

My path first took me along the top of a ridge. A strong wind blew left to right, sucking the clouds faster and faster over the top and down to the right, sometimes reducing visibility to 40 feet. Shepherds tended their flocks. Soon afterward I found myself in what appeared to be a rain forest. The path petered out. I retraced my way. In a settlement, I found a boy who would guide me through. Once free of the forest, the path reappeared. I attempted to pay the boy and say goodbye, but he motioned to me that he much preferred continuing with me—even though we couldn't communicate about where I was headed. "No," I told myself, "I want to do this on my own." I insisted on paying him and moving ahead alone. To this day, I have felt a little bad for refusing his request. I guess it would have been an adventure for him, too, perhaps to places he'd never seen. I wonder if he still remembers his short job of guiding a person whose country of origin he never knew.

As evening was about to fall, I stopped in a village and asked one of the two questions written on my scrap of paper. She nodded that she had food. As I glanced at the dirt floor, I spied a place to sleep. In the meantime, I got a bucket of hot water for my reddening foot sore. Still being daylight, a couple of townsfolk, seemingly intrigued by something, watched as I let my foot soak. After a meal as local as I've ever had, I laid down for the night. I felt like I was sleeping on an incline with my legs elevated. I guess that's one thing, along with a red foot, that hiking in the mountains will do.

Next day, I was still on my own with the map and the knowledge of how to ask two questions. I had an early version of a Sony video camera as remarkably compact as a paperback book (color but no sound). I motioned to a young woman that I'd like to shoot her. She agreed, but stood on the path rigid and motionless, not being able to understand that my camera took moving pictures. To this day, when I look at the movie, she's motionless.

The pencil line on my handwritten map did come to an end. As instructed, I turned around and started back through the mountains. As before, the path descended sharply to a bucolic stream that was being fjorded by many travelers, including porters carrying 90 pounds of cargo on their backs regardless of whether they were 30 years old or 15. As I took off my shoes and began crossing the stream, yelling caught my attention. I turned and looked just in time to see water blasting through the canyon toward our crossing point. I backtracked fast enough to avoid being swept away. I heard later that distant storms often create such a wall of water that carries away the unsuspecting or slow footed.

Within an hour or two, I was traveling through the rain forest again. An older man and a boy stood in the forest. I believe it was a grandfather teaching his grandson some lessons in life. As far as I could understand their motions, they wanted me to engage the grandson to guide me for an indeterminate amount of time. I was on my own, though, and alone I would go! This seemed to disappoint both of them. I've felt a bit bad ever since. Later, still alone, I found mangos in a village at a slightly lower elevation. Mangos upon mangos upon mangos! For sale to someone with cash. A good mango being my favorite fruit, I bought mangos (upon mangos)—30 in all at a price equal to one US cent each. I ate one (after another), maybe 10 that day, since the load was heavy.

I eventually reappeared at the starting point on my map— a small village in these Himalaya Mountains. This was the village where the mountain-savvy man, a Peace Corps volunteer from Washington State whom I was legally supposed to stay with, had said goodbye and good luck. The trip had started earlier, in Katmandu. We had talked in a funky café, and he'd asked if I'd like to visit the village where he taught school. "Why, yes. And how do we get there?" I'd asked. "Once you get permission from the government, we'll take a plane for an hour to eastern Nepal. We'll next travel by bus for two hours. To the end of the road. Then we'll hike for four days."

My new friend had won trekking permission for me, since I'd be with him and he was knowledgeable about his speck of the Himalayas. He had been trek indoctrinated. We had flown for an hour and taken a bus two hours. Next day, we'd climbed for a day to the village where the Peace Corps rented the second floor of a building. There, however, he met another Peace Corps volunteer who'd gotten ill hiking at a higher altitude and left her group to come lower. It was clear the two of them were getting along quite well. The next morning, it was agreed by all that they would go to his village of a name I never learned, and I would embark on an adventure of my own. He then scribbled out the two-phrase dictionary in Nepali and penciled a map on a scrap of paper.

That's how I'd left for parts unknown. Hiking in the Himalayas on my own has been one of the most exquisite adventures in my life and one that drifts through my mind often, from a time I was willing to fly by the seat of my pants.

I'm wondering right now why I didn't just ignore that end point on the penciled map and moved on, step after step on one trail or another, for hours, days, with places to eat, floors to collapse on, villages, people, mangos, rain forests, rivers, shepherds. Sometimes we don't snap to it, letting opportunities slip away. That one did.

Looking at a real map years later, I believe the plane from Kathmandu landed in Dharan, and the bus traveled north to Dhankuta. Back then, the places with the clouds being sucked over the ridge, the shepherds, the girl who didn't move for my video camera, the rain forest, the killer river, and the end point on the map seemed like a million miles from anywhere. But all were about equidistant from India (to the South), Bangladesh (then East Pakistan; SE), Bhutan (E), and Tibet (N), each just 40 to 60 miles away. The legendary city of Lhasa in Tibet lay 250 miles northeast.

overland to Europe

By train, cart, bus, and boat I would find my way from Nepal to the swinging door of the farmhouse my grandmother grew up in outside of Oulu, Finland. The Arctic Circle goes right through that abandoned farmhouse, leaving just a chilled trace—or so I believed (slightly wrong on that, I'd learn in Finland).

This overland journey upon leaving Nepal started with a stay in Calcutta and a train ride toward the conflict that would become the Indo-Pakistani War of 1971, which would claim 11,000 military lives. Off the train and walking north, I met a soldier—one of many who seemed to have his bearings. He agreed to guide me toward the India–East Pakistan border. Before we could get there, though, an officer intercepted us, rebuked my guide, and compelled me to make an about-face and walk due south. I didn't look back.

Lingering in India, I lamented that I had never been in a jungle. I wanted to be. I spotted one across the street during a 15-minute bus stop. It must be a universe of otherworldly green, steam rising from the living floor, I thought. I entered my first jungle! For 15 minutes. Green it was, "steaming" it was not.

Another train journey later, I was walking down the long entry-way to the Taj Mahal. Later, I found close-up views of Hindu religious rites performed half submerged in the Ganges as the most sacred of rivers, and visited a hospital in New Delhi. What could my bouts of fever alternating with chills be, was a question my guest house mom suggested I bring to a doctor. All he would say was, "Malaria is prevalent here in the capital." I left his office with pills. As I walked toward the hospital exit, I turned to go back and ask whether he knew that I had malaria or if it was just a possibility. After weaving my way through hallways filled with people sitting, lying, and waiting in distress, I thought the better of bothering the doctor for even a few more seconds. There was only one downside: as a possible malaria carrier, I wouldn't be permitted to donate blood for quite some time.

• • •

I had the bread to keep traveling since a generous school loan in Minneapolis left me with a $2,000 pile of cash. My expenses were manageable, averaging $3.37 a day in the last 12 countries. At $640, the cost of a plane ticket was a blow, but it did land me in ten countries between LA and India.

Meanwhile, my traveling companion Tom Woxland did not find a freighter to Australia. On Christmas Day he jumped instead on an Israeli boat, leaving Yokohama for the South China Sea, Indian Ocean, and Red Sea—with stops in Hong Kong, Singapore, Djibouti, and two Ethiopian ports. It was a 40-day voyage on a small and ancient pre-war freighter. He'd live for nine months on the citrus and poultry kibbutz Kfar Menachem, between Tel Aviv and Jerusalem. Just a kilometer away lay the ancient Philistine city of Gath, home of Goliath. He'd return for many subsequent stays.

• • •

As for me, I was outta India over the border to West Pakistan in a horse cart. After visits to Lahore and Peshawar, I boarded a third-class bus through the famed Khyber Pass into Afghanistan. A young army officer in Kabul befriended me and gave me a tour of a surprising botanical garden with thousands of colorful flowers blooming in this dry mountain land. I then hooked my way by land southerly and westerly through the cities of Kandahar and Herat. Why were the boys on the dusty street in Herat throwing stones at me? I'll never know. I did shield myself from these rocks that must have carried some message in the boys' minds. Perhaps it was spelled F-U-N.

Little did I know back then that these grounds, with loose stones and my own footsteps, may have been crossed by my father's father's father to the nth degree and his wife, siblings, and cousins. That was 40,000 years ago, partway through my lineage's journey of perhaps 3,000 generations from Africa to Finland (and ultimately to my hometown of Biwabik, Minnesota).[6]

After uncountable hours of sleeping on the bus from Afghanistan to Iran, I sought out a doctor in the capital of Tehran. First, though, I checked into a hotel and had a hard time waking myself up at 4 p.m. to get to the doc's office. I explained that I was nearly always fast asleep. He had just the solution for me, a prescription for pills. I dutifully took them, but only slept longer. Somewhere along the way between Iran and Turkey, a British medical student on his own adventure read the French labeling on my pill bottle. He pointed out the French word for insomnia, written in black and white. The doctor had misunderstood me to say I could not sleep. After stopping the medication, I started feeling alive to the world again.

---

[6] This journey of my lineage is discussed later, in "A Brief History of Traveling Genes."

meandering in Europe

The trip that was supposed to last six months was now in its four-teenth month, going on the fifteenth. I began meandering slightly faster, through Esram, Ankara, and Istanbul in Turkey, Athens and Greek Islands, Yugoslavia, Romania, West Germany, Venice, and creeping around the Adriatic shores to Barcelona in Spain. I next made it to the sea in Hamburg, Germany, to board an overnight ship to Helsinki. Partying with a seaman in his quarters, I was surprised he'd fling an empty drinking glass against the door of his cabin, watch it shatter, and calmly sweep the shards into a dust pan. I was also surprised to see the crew hurl plastic bagfuls of garbage into the sea in the dead of night.

Taking a train from Helsinki to the north of Finland, I made it to the ancestral home of my father's parents in Oulu, meeting cousins who showed me the now-abandoned farm home that my grandmother Matilda left for America. As my feet crossed the home's threshold, I knew that the last person with any American connection stepping on it was my grandmother, who had left as a Finnish citizen, never to return. I tread gently, completing a family circle. Later traveling to Rovaniemi and taking a bus north from downtown, I asked to get off at the five-mile point. All alone up there, I picked two handfuls of blueberries in the low sun of an early October afternoon—blueberries ripening smack on the Arctic Circle.

Four hours south of that imaginary line around a skinny part of the globe, I found beautiful farming land around Ilmajoki. It was here that I stopped and wandered, wondering what life was like for my mother's parents. Today, all the Ilmajoki relatives who we know of live in places like northern Ohio, northern California, Minnesota, and Thunder Bay, Ontario.

I then returned to Italy to meet a friend, Marline, who had flown over the Atlantic from Minnesota to join me. Marline and I wished to visit the Vatican and the Sistine Chapel. Her skirt, however hip for the times, was too short for the Vatican. Entry denied. Outside, she was able to tug it down. On our second attempt, we gained access. The frescoes "introduce visitors into the world of the Revelation," the Vatican informed us.

Marline volunteered to carry smoked reindeer meat from my Finnish relatives back to the USA, since I would not be getting home for some weeks yet. Before arriving in America, she stashed it inside the clothes she was wearing, just in case importing reindeer meat wasn't legal. That worked. I later shared it with my Minnesota uncles, aunts, and cousins, telling them about our close relatives who never emigrated from Finland and the now-abandoned farmhouse Matilda said goodbye to in 1899.

My world trip of 1970–71 didn't end in the Vatican or with handing Marline the reindeer meat, however. The homestretch meant I had to make my way to London. In the way stood Munich's Oktoberfest —Germany's most visited party—and Cologne's cathedral—the country's most visited landmark, whose construction began in 1248 and ended without completion in 1473. A note on a London hostel bulletin board touting Machu Picchu in Peru soon stared me in the face. New worlds are out there to explore, I understood. Fifteen years later, I still had that note in mind as I headed to South America. That first time, I barely knew a single word of Spanish, but I'd make more trips as years passed.[7]

Meanwhile, sixteen months after I'd left Minneapolis for LA in my VW Bug, I crossed the Atlantic by jet and landed in New York City.[8]

---

[7] I bring these trips back to life again in "South America," a bit later in this book.

[8] What I experienced in the New York City of 1971 is touched on in "Tales of Strange in a Large City."

MESOAMERICA

MEXICO

Speaking the Languages and Carrying Big Sticks
APRIL 4, 2004

"Don't go outside tonight!" I am warned.

"Why?" I inquire.

"You'll get bitten by the dog," is the answer.

Is that true, or are secret dangers lurking in the total darkness? I wonder. A thousand visitors flood the locale during the day. Few, if any, sleep overnight. After being shut in a shed for 12 hours, I find the morning tranquil and not yet invaded by visitors.

Mexico's most beautiful waterfall lies in the semitropical mountains of Southern Mexico. A river divides into two to create slender islands with cascading steps of water along the islands' sides, before the rejoined river falls with a roar that can be heard all night, even in sheds for shut-in visitors. Nine ropes strung across the river in the almost-safe-for-swimming pool below the big falls may catch you if you've ventured in upriver and have survived the tumbles. Lifeguards lounge around in street clothes, talking to friends and gazing at the river, ready to throw out a roped tube. Agua Azul—"blue water"—is the official name for the falls. Yesterday, after a typical torrential rain, the color was chocolate. This morning it was green.

Boys in this bit of Chiapas State habitually carry sticks. Not just a run-of-the-mill stick, but one that has a distinctive shape and size. Some boys—it appears—do not modify nature's creations, while others—to satisfy a human creative impulse—contour the ends just so. Why they're carried, I wasn't sure. Not for protection, it seemed, except for the shed owner who guided me across a big field from the only store open last night back to my room. When the dog howled ferociously, he picked up a large stick from the ground. Although I couldn't see—it was dark—I think he then picked up another for his other hand and confronted the dog. Or rather two dogs.

"How many languages do you speak?" I like to ask people in multicultural communities. Julio, the seven-year-old at the store, speaks the regional Mayan language of Tzeltal and answered my questions in Spanish (with the help of his mother). The two-stick defender knows three languages. The boys who sweep the walks at Agua Azul with worn brooms speak little Spanish.

As the thousand visitors begin to trickle in, I jet out of Agua Azul in a van, enjoying five hours on curvy mountain roads back to the central town of San Cristóbal de Las Casas. "This Is The Zapatista Territory of the Rebellion" announces a sign on the way. Valuable natural resources abound in Chiapas, but the people are among Mexico's poorest. The Zapatista Army of National Liberation (EZLN), founded in 1983 and composed mostly of young indigenous people of Chiapas, took armed control of San Cristóbal de las Casas and four other cities on January 1, 1994. After 12 days of deadly fighting, the Mexican army regained control. The EZLN fought, and still advocates, for land redistribution and greater political and cultural autonomy for the indigenous people. The response of the Mexican government has fallen far short of these demands.

The EZLN has, nevertheless, been the "most powerful political [rebel group] in Mexico in nearly 100 years," journalist Paulina Vargas recently noted.[9] Still, "being an indigenous person [in Mexico] means being treated as half a person, and if you are a woman, even less so," stated Maria de Jesús Patricio Martinez, a Zapatista-endorsed Nahua who was a 2018 presidential candidate.[10]

---

[9] Paulina Vargas, "In a Mexico 'Tired of Violence,' Rebels Give Politics a Try," *New York Times,* August 27, 2017, A6.

[10] Ibid.

Life in the territory indeed appears to be precarious. Along the road throughout the territory of the recent rebellion, the cliff edge is washed down and out at many points. Men work to repair one washout, carrying buckets of wet cement on their shoulders and scooping rocks into other pails to pour in the gaping hole. At another washout, where a truck driver didn't realize the road had disappeared, hundreds of pieces of lumber slid down the cliff. There, men and boys yanking ropes pulled the boards up the cliff one at a time. At another spot, all traffic was stopped as a wrecker tried without success to pull a bus back onto the highway. Of the hundreds of accidents you see waiting to happen, only a few actually occur. Much to my relief, I made it out unscathed.

Dreams in San Cristóbal de las Casas
APRIL 6, 2004

In San Cristóbal de las Casas, at 9,000 feet, I'm out of breath. Am I, however, back in "civilization?" I guess so. A lady at the tourist office readily marked on my map where I could catch the all-night bus to the next part of Mexico, Oaxaca. "What time does it leave?" I inquired. To answer that question, she called over a coworker. He dug around in her drawer to find the schedule. She then admired her remarkably red fingernails and with a laugh let her coworkers in on the reason she couldn't hunt in the drawer herself: she'd painted her fingernails on the job, and they were too wet to dig for information.

One night here in San Cristóbal, I had a dream—or was it a dream —that I was sleeping in a monastery—or was it a hacienda or a museum? Out my window next to the fireplace was a pine forest—or was it a flower garden or vegetable garden? When I woke up I realized that all of this was somewhat true. The building was first a monastery and later a private hacienda. After it was left abandoned to deteriorating elements, a Swiss journalist-photographer and her Danish archaeologist husband who'd met in the jungle came upon it some 60 or 70 years ago. They

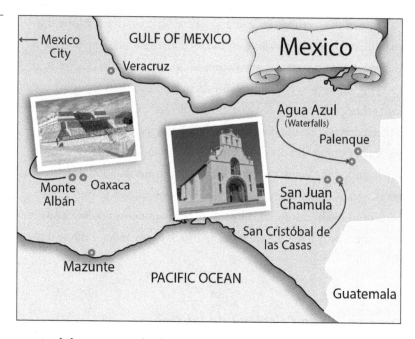

Mexico City — | GULF OF MEXICO | **Mexico**

Veracruz

Agua Azul (Waterfalls)

Palenque

Monte Albán   Oaxaca

San Juan Chamula

San Cristóbal de las Casas

Mazunte   PACIFIC OCEAN

Guatemala

repaired the premises, built guest rooms for visitors, and called it home for decades. It's now a museum-library-lodge-restaurant-pine forest-garden of one's dreams called Casa Na Bolom.

The Swiss-Danish couple documented the cultural traditions of the Lacandon Maya and others and were intent on helping to preserve the people's customs and their natural resources. The Lacandon lived in an inaccessible rain forest untouched by the rest of the world until the 1940s. About a thousand people speak Lacandon today. It's one of the 31 groups totaling about six million Maya people in Mexico, Guatemala, and Belize that speak different, mutually unintelligible languages.

My breakfast waiter at Casa Na Bolom was Angel, a Lacandon studying in San Cristóbal, eight hours by bus from home. He and the cooks welcomed a photo I shot of them in the kitchen of the monastery-hacienda-museum-lodge-dream maker. This was the exception to the rule. Photos are strictly disallowed in many of the indigenous villages of Chiapas where residents, understandably keen to keep their soul, fear you might steal it from them with a snapshot. You may ask. But expect to be turned down.

Mexico's Biwabik
APRIL 15, 2008

Mazunte, on the Pacific Coast of Mexico, is a pint-sized Biwabik, Minnesota, home to 500 residents rather than 800. A British traveler in the know confided to me last year that Mazunte is one of his four favorite places in Mexico. (I listen to suggestions, opinions, and travails.) It's now one of my favorite places too, but don't spread the word! Let tranquil Mazunte keep being its true self.

Kids living in Mazunte like to slide on sand or water as much as Minnesotans like to slide down winter hills. Kids walk to the beach in the bay that Mazunte has all to itself. They fling boogie boards down on the wet beach sand, jump on the board as it's moving, slide to the ocean's edge, then dive, jump, or fall into the next wave to hit the shore. They like this as much as coming toward shore on their boogie board stomachs.

"Hey, you kids, can an adult succeed on a boogie board or only kids?" I ask them. One opines that an adult can do it. As if to prove his point, he hands me his board. He is right. I surf in on my stomach successfully. But what do you do when the big wave you're riding breaks hard onto the beach? If you're like me, you go head over heels, or thrice versa, and feel a water punch in the face as if you mistakenly got in a boxing ring. Right then, my brain's eye saw an MRI of my entire nasal cavity system, but enlarged by six times. I didn't know that system was so complex and that water under pressure would fill every bit of it.

Lost in Time and Space
APRIL 19, 2008

One day, hours from Mazunte, I was lost in time and space. Sitting on the ground, I shut my eyes for quite some time. When I opened them, I was still surrounded by the first true city in Mesoamerica, Monte Albán, in the Southern Mexican state of Oaxaca. Still there for the eyes to behold are pyramids, temples, ball courts, grand stairways, and perhaps an astronomical observatory. Hidden underneath is a web of tunnels. We don't know what the tunnels were for, but wouldn't it have been mysterious for a priest to disappear from one colorful and smoky temple, only to reappear a thousand feet away in another temple? Some have so speculated.

Hunters and gatherers roamed the Oaxaca Valley 15,000 years ago. Many thousands of years later, they built settlements. Around 500 B.C., another culture started building Monte Albán, moving millions of tons of rock and earth to level a mountain top. It was set a thousand feet above the productive valley floor, far from sources of water and food. (Within hours, I'd return to the valley floor due to hunger and thirst.)

Then about 800 A.D., Monte Albán, by then a city of some 20,000 inhabitants, was mysteriously abandoned. Mysterious it is to us, but the people certainly knew why they were leaving. They must have left by the dozen, not thousand, I decided sitting atop a pyramid, contemplating. Your guess is as good as mine and those of many other experts, for we're still not sure of the answer. (By 2019, however, evidence pointed to a surprise attack. So perhaps the people departed by the ten thousand!)

The Houses of Worship

APRIL 23, 2008

If you make your way to San Juan Chamula, not far from bustling San Cristóbal de las Casas in Chiapas State, keep your camera under wraps and turned off, or you might be mistaken for a soul robber. Besides, outsiders are viewed with suspicion, since few have ever brought any good with them. In 1524, the Spanish invaders forced their way into town with the help of some conniving inhabitants from the next village. Or so I'm told. The Roman Catholic Church took hold in the neighboring village, but not here in Chamula.

Today, a Catholic priest seldom visits Chamula because most of the marriage, funeral, and other ceremonies are performed at home. Those who have been converting to Evangelicalism or Mormonism in recent years are not welcome, either. They have been forced out of town, it's said, and many moved miles away. I did not make myself unwelcome since I kept my camera out of sight and treaded quietly in the places I'm about to describe.

Do engage a guide trusted by the people of Chamula. What we have over in that backyard, I surmise, is a family party about to kick off before noon on Saturday. They haven't quite finished the laundry since they are hanging it out to dry under the pure bright sky at 7,200 feet. Kids are playing. It's as simple as that!

Or is it a party? No. Today is the last day of the 20-day Maya month. The man sitting in the white robe behind the table of laundry tubs full of water and clothing is a religious leader. The clothing drapes the statues of saintly deities populating local homes and is usually washed in the river. Piece by piece, a woman lifts an item of dripping clothing out of the wash pan and hands it to a man, who walks to the clothesline and hangs it. Another piece is given to another man, and he hangs it. In this way, the saints will be dressed in the purest of clothing.

On the edge of town, what we have is a Catholic church in ruins and a cemetery with hundreds of crosses. The white ones mark children's graves. The church burned a hundred years ago. The official story is that fireworks accidentally ignited the roof. A hushed revelation counters that the people of Chamula did not appreciate the Christian beliefs and customs forced upon them. Then the church caught fire.

In the middle of town, what we have is a Catholic church on the site of an ancient indigenous temple. But what am I hearing? Someone says it is Catholic on the outside only. As we enter, we walk on a bed of pine needles strewn across the expansive floor—so we're not stepping directly on the underworld. The church bells and the statues of Catholic saints that were transferred here a hundred years ago from the frowned-upon burned church are set against a wall. The clothing covering these particular saints is rather dirty: no one in town is inclined to take it to the river or a backyard to be washed. The locally revered indigenous saints in this temple of worship, though, are draped in freshly cleaned garb.

This house of worship has no pews. What it does have is 30 wooden tables lining the walls and crowding the altar area. Over 2,000 candles stand on these tables and the floor. Every candle is burning. Family groups sit on the floor here and there, speaking the Tzotzil Mayan language, and the older long-haired women are chanting. The candles lit in front of them commemorate those who have passed on. One family group has brought a live hen, and an older woman performs a ritual of sacrifice. She stretches the hen's neck, like pulling hard on each end of a short length of rope to get the kinks out. Once dead, the hen is laid on the floor in front of the group.

Not far away, a man and woman are, like most parishioners, seated on the floor. He is chanting, with 150 burning candles divided into six rows sticking to the floor in front of them. By consulting a worshipper scraping candle wax off the floor and brushing pine needles away from burning candles, I learn more about the man and woman. The man, I am told in a whisper, is a *curandero* (shaman, or medicine man), and the woman seated next to him is ill, perhaps with a blood ailment. He is helping to cure her, charging $15 or more per session. The sessions are lengthy. I notice that he is wearing a jacket made of sheep's wool, which costs over 3,000 pesos, or $300.

I ask the wax-scraping whisperer about another man, too: "What is that man's title, the one with a heavily smoking incense container, waving it back and forth in front of every statue of the many saints?" He is a *mayordomo*, I learn. I would have asked about mayordomos, but I knew the whisperer had tasks to perform, and my unspoken question wisps away in a cloud of smoke. (Months after that smoke cleared, I learned that a mayordomo is one appointed to perform many ceremonial and religious duties, including looking after two or more saints.)

The people of San Juan Chamula expect to practice their religion, which echoes some aspects of Christianity, well into the future. A 24-year-old has just added his name to the list of those who'll be selected to be church leaders for one year. He'll have to wait his turn, for the list is long. He believes his turn will come when he is 56 years old. Will he then become a mayordomo?

As I left San Juan Chamula for San Cristóbal de las Casas by van, my eyes stuck to everything I saw out the window, and my mind settled softly on what I'd learned and the people whose paths I'd crossed. I'd want to go back again and again. And I did.

A Special Star in the Heavens
APRIL 22, 2008

In San Cristóbal de las Casas, I'm planning to have lunch with K'an Joy Chitam II. His lineage gave splendor to the majestic Maya city of Palenque in Southern Mexico. Palenque, embraced on all sides by a jungle of beasts, exoticism, and magic, fought rival city Tonina to control the commercial route from the Gulf of Mexico to the heart of the Maya empire.

K'an Joy Chitam II is known as one of the most brilliant leaders in history. When newly widowed, Tonina's ruler Kawil, or Smoked Mirror, dressed in the military robes of her late husband to command her people's attention and resolved to attack Palenque. The Tonina warriors did not take Palenque but managed to capture the God-Ruler K'an Joy Chitam II (who I'll call "Kan Joy"). To further humiliate the people of Palenque, Kawil then unmasked herself: their ruler Kan Joy had been captured by a woman!

I understand that in his cell in Tonina, Kan Joy practiced the sacred sacrifice of bloodletting by cutting himself. He hoped that the smoke that rose from the burning of his blood would bring the gods' attention to his plight. In his hallucinations, he descended to Xibalba, the Maya underworld. After Kan Joy suffered for 10 years, the Divine Twins— the sons of Heart of Heaven and Heart of Earth—took pity on him and sent the Lord of the Winds to his rescue. Kan Joy returned to Palenque, where he was welcomed with great honors. Aware of his advancing age, however, he placed his nephew on the throne in his stead.

Do I know this because Kan Joy explained it to me chapter and verse before I suggested we have lunch today? Not exactly. A few nights ago, this story was reenacted, to the delight of a full house at Theater Zabadua in San Cristóbal de las Casas. Kan Joy was alive on the stage, brought back in the person of Mario Chambor. Afterward, Mario and I arranged to have this lunch. But as I seem to know Kan Joy much better than Mario, in my mind Kan Joy is the one who'll soon be sharing a meal with me.

I'm now concerned, however. The theater program says that after placing his nephew on the throne, Kan Joy set an example of wisdom, humility, and compassion by offering his life to the gods in a ritual self-sacrifice. He was then transformed into a star in the heavens, there to reign over the cosmos. So this may be a lunch I have quite alone, far beneath a special star in the heavens.

GUATEMALA

An Early Message from Guatemala

APRIL 7, 2006

Guatemala City: In Central America's biggest city, a boy who collects bus fares jumps off at a downtown stop with an empty plastic Pepsi bottle. Running to the front wheel, he remedies the problem of a missing lug nut by screwing the mouth of the bottle onto the threads where the nut went missing. Should I have given him my Coke bottle for another nut missing? Or would I have been embroiled in a lawsuit that might arise after the next turn in the road?

I'm now in the Maya town of San Pedro la Laguna on Lake Atitlán. After dark, I come across kids on a trail. They'd set up a candlelit stand, selling oranges and bananas. I buy a banana for 50 centavos, or 7 cents. They entice me to try an orange slice for free. They have only one orange on the table, but I notice a fresh stock in the tree above them. I'd soon believe that each orange grown in town was different— sweeter or more sour than the one before, juicier or pulpier. But all are fresh, some picked just seconds earlier.

Outside the internet café where I'm now typing, people have covered the cobblestone street with fresh pine needles hauled down from a volcano's slopes by a designated group of church members. Others are making designs on the bed of needles with hundreds of flower petals . . . *And now please excuse an interruption of my message about pine needles and flower petals* . . . Two girls, 11 and 12, dressed in traditional Maya Tzutujil clothing, are watching me type over my shoulder. They read the numbers 11 and 12—and know I'm writing

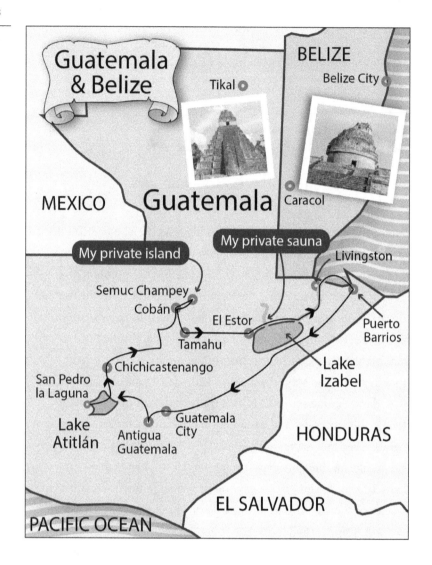

Guatemala & Belize

Tikal ○

BELIZE

Belize City ○

MEXICO

Guatemala

Caracol ○

My private sauna

My private island

Livingston

Semuc Champey

Cobán

El Estor

Tamahu

Puerto Barrios

Chichicastenango

Lake Izabel

San Pedro la Laguna

Lake Atitlán

Antigua Guatemala

Guatemala City

HONDURAS

EL SALVADOR

PACIFIC OCEAN

about them since I'd asked their ages. They also comment on how I can keep typing as we cast smiles back and forth.

Now six girls crowd around. I invite them to say something to you. *"San Pedro es muy bonito"*—San Pedro is very pretty—they tell you. One of the girls' families owns the Hotel Maritza, they say, and it has a very *"buena vista del lago"*—a great view of the lake. They are wearing *blusas*—blouses; multicolored *delantal* and *corte*—skirt and fancy apron; a *faja*—like a wide woven belt; and *caites*—sandals. I confess one of them reached over to type the Spanish words above. Their first language is *Tzutujil* (also spelled Tz'utujil), the local Mayan language which at least 95% of townspeople speak. Almost all are also fluent in Spanish.

Now back to the *alfombras*, or carpets of pine needles, flowers, and assorted vegetables lying on the street. It is Holy Thursday of *Semana Santa*, Holy Week. By evening, two or three streets will be covered. At 7 p.m., a religious procession brought to Guatemala by the Spanish in the 1500s will solemnly kick off at the Catholic church.

Children in the Western Highlands of Guatemala between Lake Atitlán and Guatemala City.

Since I've been tapping keys, the church parishioners have made surprising progress on the alfombra outside, red and yellow flower petals predominating.

• • •

It's evening now. Hundreds have left the church and shuffle forward in a slow procession on the alfombras. They're accompanied by the mournful music of horns and a trailing drum corps. Towering over the procession is a life-size figure of Christ bearing the cross, affixed to a platform shouldered by 12 men. Others swing incense cans, filling the street with smoke. Passersby take care not to trod on the alfombras until the procession has come and gone.

Minutes later, I greet an elderly man sitting on the narrow sidewalk. He invites me to join him. He doesn't hear many of my few words because he's hard of hearing.

"My name is Luis Gonzalez Chaviroc," he says in Spanish, his second language.

"My name is Tomás Mattson," I respond.

He asks my age and how old I think he is.

"Seventy," I say.

He waves it off. He is 81.

"Where you live in the United States, are the houses many floors high?" he asks.

"No, I live in a house with one floor. But in Chicago and New York, some are 80 stories high."

He's surprised. "How do they put them together so they'll withstand an earthquake?" he wonders.

I think a minute. "Metal and engineers and documents," I say.

"When I was a little kid of eight," he says, "houses were made of adobe. Do you know adobe? The roofs were thatched. Now look at all the concrete block houses."

Luis asks me to write my name on a scrap of paper he's just picked up off the street in front of us. "You don't have to write my name," he tells me, "because it is easy—Luis Gonzalez Chaviroc—but your name is *something else*." He imparts information about the world and God.

Eventually I say, "Nice to meet you, Luis." Then I walk a block past three alfombras to an internet café where I write this message about an evening on the streets.

As sure-footed as I can, I later move down a precipitously steep street and fall asleep in the shack I've been able to call my own for a month now. I hope I'll see Luis Gonzalez Chaviroc again and again.

Sipfuls and Eyefuls
MARCH 1, 2008

I'm wondering how many people walk by my shack in San Pedro la Laguna every day. I'd guess 600. I may count a more exact number in random five-minute periods someday and multiply exponentially.

Why not trod on the seven-foot-wide trail of hyperpulverized volcanic sand that runs by my shack? Within a minute, an old man named Antonio gives me a wonderfully common greeting: *"Buenos días."* Antonio is carrying a machete. He's heading up the volcanic slope outside town to cut coffee, he informs me. I saw Antonio yesterday, too, as I walked home at 7 a.m. with a mug of coffee fetched three blocks away. He wondered what my mug held, and I handed it to him. He sipped. He made a little face and handed it back. "More?" I inquired. No, it seemed one sip of strong coffee without sugar was enough.

Antonio bravely taking that sip is just the tip of the iceberg. I peeked into Freedom Bar one night when a live band blared. I went in because I'd just seen short-statured Antonio, in his local clothes head to toe, slip in despite being pushed around by even more eager and much taller young people, the non-Maya big city *"ladinos."* The bar was filled with dancers in their 20s and 30s from Guatemala City. They've discovered that this laid-back town is a great destination for the national holiday break of Holy Week. Antonio took the measure of everything happening—the musicians singing in Spanish about love and marijuana, the dancers' body moves and steps, their utter exuberance. Antonio is the kind of man with the verve to get sipfuls and eyefuls.

I happen to know just the place Antonio can find endless sipfuls he'll love. I'll urge him to try a mocha, macchiato, or cappuccino. I'll stick to black coffee—with no sugar—for the purity of it all. Antonio might have harvested some of these beans himself—up the volcanic slope at a perfect altitude and in the perfect amount of shade. His beans are part of a prime coffee harvest from up to 300 growers— every bean bought at a premium price. Just before roasting, they'll be inspected again by Jose Luis Gonzalez, owner of the Café Las Cristalinas, a coffeehouse of growing fame.

On the path again—another day and new eyefuls and earfuls. Masons are working on a new restaurant. They're building a wood form so they can pour concrete steps to the second floor. "What is that form called?" I ask. *"Una forma?"*

"No, *una molda*," they answer. The construction workers stop what they're doing and converse. They are from San Pablo, a town within sight just a few miles down the lakeshore.

I hear a softly spoken *"Amigo, ayuda"*—help, my friend. It comes from an eight-year-old on his knees with his bicycle. "Yes, I can help you," I answer. He's on his way to school, which starts soon and is far away. His bike chain has slipped off, and his hands are covered in chain oil. I bend down. I don't tell him that I might be inept: the last time I put a chain back on a bike was when I was 10. The two of us are determined, though. On the second try, it stays on. We pull leaves off bushes and wipe our hands.

"Amigo," a woman in the local Maya dress says softly, just like the boy on the bike. She motions ever so slightly to the big wash pan she's balancing on a fence post. A towel conceals what's inside. She may be the one who comes around selling hot tamales covered with a cloth.

Before I can say, "Yes, I'd like one or two," I realize from another ever so slight motion that she wants me to lift the heavy pan to the top of her head. Now I see it's a load of wet clothes she's just washed in the lake.

An acquaintance silently takes me onto private property. He leads me to a small stone altar he believes is 500 years old. Few ever see it. We aren't supposed to be here, either. As we talk about the animal sacrifice practice of old, the landowner arrives to feed the pigs. We stay hidden. Will we die of old age at a sacrificial altar? We eventually slink away through neighboring coffee farms. I haven't told anyone about the sacred spot. It's a well-kept secret.

I walk two blocks to ask a French man married to a San Pedro woman a question that's been nagging me. Song fills their yard. A little girl and boy are each holding ends of garden hoses up to their mouths—a microphone for each of them! For good measure, they've now climbed up several steps and look down at me from their stage. I ask if they are singing for me, for the neighbors, or for the whole

Contingent of festive celebrants on a parade day in San Pedro la Laguna.

world. They are singing for me! After the first song, they tell me they have a second. I stay for the concert. I leave, forgetting what question I came to ask.

Along the trail comes the Maya boy in red lipstick. A girl who sells glasses of freshly made orange juice once told me there is such a boy. "Is this acceptable?" I ask her.

"No."

"Who says?" I inquire.

"Says the municipal officials at a community meeting."

"Who told them to say it's not acceptable?" I demand to know.

She puzzled over this question, then pronounces that "the president" says so.

The boy now walks on the streets frequently, sometimes with a friend without lipstick. Townsfolk don't seem concerned. Perhaps the new president has new priorities.

As time goes by, I may see the boy with the unchained bicycle, hands oily black and calling, "Amigo, ayuda." I may see a woman with a wash pan simply saying, "Amigo." I may see girls and boys singing, but probably not holding the ends of garden hoses to their mouths. The boy in lipstick may walk by on his way to meet his friend. I may see the construction workers pouring *cemento* into *moldas*, willing to teach me words from the world of construction. And among hundreds of others on the streets, trails, and lake, all going about particular missions, I'll surely see Antonio on his way to the coffee hills, or maybe checking into the frenetic nightlife of visitors to this centuries-old Maya town in the mountains.

A Return to My Shack
JANUARY 29, 2009

I've settled in for another stay in my shack in San Pedro la Laguna. Coming here, I was weighted down by screwdrivers, teaspoons, a stapler, sheets, Cuba travel guides, hot pads, and a fan that'll blow hot air out from under my tin roof.

I'm hearing all sorts of garden-variety advice in Spanish from several San Pedro people and in English from a French man and a Canadian gardener extraordinaire, David Taylor. Slice the top half off the jasmine tree and beautiful flowers will abound. Pull the vines off the orange trees so the tips of the parasites won't pierce the oranges, suck them dry, and kill whole branches. Cut that bunch of 80 bananas off when the first one starts to turn yellow or the birds will peck at them. Move your slat fence a foot in so it's not encroaching on an absent and sensitive neighbor's property. Repair the plank fence on the other end so kids can't climb in. Pull the oranges off the tree with your long pole before they get too ripe and fall to the ground. Get rid of the rotting oranges on the ground. And prune the branches of the nispero tree so the fruits can ripen.

"What is a nispero?" a Chicago friend once asked.

"It's a strawberry-sized fruit with a flavor all its own," I answered, "just like every other fruit in the world. I've never known two different kinds of fruits to have the same flavor, have you? I believe it's been that way ever since the Garden of Eden."

I hear over time that I could snip leaves off the orange tree to make tea that'll treat a cough. I could wrap my torso in banana leaves, put a shirt on, and go to bed for the night for a stomach ache. I could strap slices of potatoes to my forehead with a bandana, and my headache will disappear.

"Do you do these things?" I ask.

The composite answer I've received: "No, most people now go to a pharmacy or doctor, but a grandparent may indeed employ tried and true remedies."

As I am painstakingly moving the slat fence one foot in with my neighbor Pedro, his son Diego shows up to help. The working language suddenly changes from Spanish to Tzutujil, but they still speak Spanish to me. "Do you have any cooking oil, Tomás?" they ask. I don't. Short of new nails, we hammer rusty bent ones straighter. They'd penetrate the wood more smoothly, of course, if we coated them with cooking oil.

Up in town at the Sunday market, I sit down in the shade. There's only room for so many people, and we're all there. Little boys and girls are resting from basketball games they play on the court. We talk about Cuba, Obama, and healthy fruits and vegetables. "How many of you have ever talked to a foreigner before?" I ask. For three of five of them, I'm the first foreigner they've talked to. People have no idea, of course, where I'm from. They might guess Germany, *Holanda*, Australia, or the US.

One of the girls in Tzutijil clothing is squeezed up against me, eating a choco-banano on a Popsicle stick. It's popular in town—chocolate-covered banana. A boy has a chocolate-covered something else. After he licks off the chocolate, I see it's a choco-melon. Another has a round choco-something else; I now see it's a choco-mandarina. One who's eaten the chocolate off a choco-sandia—watermelon—gives me a couple bites of the sandia. I coin a word for them to cover all their choco-fruits—"choco-fruta."

Joe, whom I met on a trail, quit his job as an economist in New York City after 50 weeks, but not before, in his boredom, he used pens and pencils of all colors and dozens of white-out bottles to create wonderful works of art on every size Post-It that his firm stocked. I scrolled through 81 of them on his touch-screen iPod music player. A New York City art gallery will exhibit his work next month.

"Meantime," I tell Joe, "you can paint whatever you want on any wall in my shack, since all I've got up are jeans and shirts hanging from rusty nails pounded into walls of fading colors." He comes over, sits on a stool inside, and studies the place. "A shack it is," Joe concludes.

The walls continue to fade. Joe the economist apparently prefers Post-Its.

Kite on a String without End

A Note to Friend Dan MacMeekin
MARCH 23, 2010

Hi Dan,

Yes, Dan, Guatemala is cheering me up! Cuba is a challenge. I think I bit off too much to chew—staying for all 30 days of my visa, walking for miles in 10 cities, and searching endlessly for jugs of water and fresh fruits. After coming back to Guatemala, I sat in my yard, silently staring straight ahead for a long time.

Compared to Cuba, life is very different where I hang out here. I can't remember if I had a plan of what to do today. If so, I can't cross anything off that lost to-do list. A friend showed up at 8 a.m. and wanted us to work in my yard. I agreed. But at 4 p.m., we realized we hadn't done a lick of work and decided to go swimming instead. Part of our time together had been spent buying fruits and vegetables in the market. At the shack, we sliced a loaf of whole grain bread and picked the sandwich we desired: Wisconsin cheese, mashed potatoes, and Guatemalan red peppers, tomatoes, and guacamole. We took the time—because we had the time—to blend a *licuado* of milk, yogurt, pineapple, and bananas. The dishes got washed with a hose in the yard. Realizing it was 4 p.m. and time for a swim, we packed a few mangos. At the lake, I neither understood nor really needed to know anything he said in Tzutujil to his friends.

After a day that floated outward like a kite on a string without end,
I may shy away from the wasted effort of making plans or lists.

Ciao, Tom

Voyage to My Private Island
APRIL 16, 2010

You've heard about an island. You don't know its name. If you can find
it, you tell yourself, you'll relax on top of it surrounded by towering
flowers. You may be the first person ever to do so. The island may be
untouched by human hands.

You grab what you need from a shack covered by a corrugated
tin roof and take a fast *lancha* across the lake of unknown depth.
At Panajachel, you hop onto one bus after another and bed down in
Chichicastenango on a Saturday night. No one said it would be a
picnic getting to your private island.

Just before sundown, you walk to cemetery hill. The gate is locked
because it's already after hours. A boy on a bicycle directs you to a
half-hidden gate that's open, though. You welcome the idea that you'll
be the only person in the centuries-old cemetery. But once deep inside,
you come across several people at a family gravesite, and then more at
another, each group burning candles, talking, and hugging one another.
One couple is in tears.

In the evening, you walk up, down, and sideways on the steep
stone steps that fan out from the blackened door of the Santo Tomás
Church, built sometime during the 1700s. In the darkness, two men
swing cans of smoking incense toward the burning candles outside
the broad church door, which has become ever more scorched century
after century. Take time to count the steps. They correspond to the
18 months in the primary Maya calendar.

The next morning, dozens of candles burn in several spots inside
Santo Tomás Church. A couple kneeling just inside the entrance is

engaged in a long dialogue as their candles sparkle on a low platform sprinkled with flower petals. They may be paying respects to ancestors and saints, or praying for someone they know who is in need. More often, though, one is a Maya priest engaged by the other.

A service of a different kind, a Catholic service, begins at 8 a.m. Mass is in both Spanish and K'iche' (formerly spelled Quiché). The priest names dozens of parishioners who are ill, traveling, or mourning the loss of a loved one, and they are thus remembered. All the while, the dialogue of the couple at the back continues. We are having two services at once, befitting this sacred setting that held a Maya temple before waves of Spaniards came along, bearing a foreign religion.

Your mind wanders to something you've learned in recent days. The K'iche' Maya, for perhaps much longer than a thousand years, have embraced a belief about how earth and life were created from just a calm sea and a sky devoid of life. The beliefs also explain human history, which perhaps began in this vicinity. For the spellbinding details, you'll have to read the Popol Vuh, sometimes called the Maya Bible—or alternatively, a book description or an online summary.

The story, first oral, is said to have been written down in K'iche' by a Maya scribe in the 1550s. It was treasured by the people here in Chichicastenango but has been lost, perhaps burned by Catholic priests along with thousands of Maya codices full of images. Prior to its loss, a Spanish priest who'd gained the trust of the community had translated the K'iche' text into Spanish (and perhaps relied on oral telling). For three centuries, the Spanish text was kept hidden in this church. The Newberry Library in Chicago has it now.

As the parishioners kneel, you quietly take leave. Attending a Catholic service, let alone kneeling, is not part of your personal history. Gone now are the candles at the back and the couple in conversation. It's a shame you won't be in town long enough to find out how the prayers are answered.

A bus takes you all the way to Pachalum within a few short hours. You discover there's no public transportation to Granados in the next province. Fortunately, you bump into a hardware store owner who owns a 1980 four-cylinder Nissan pickup. The fact that it's short on brake fluid, water, and gas is remedied. After 75 minutes driving over nearly every rock on the narrow road, you find yourself sitting on a curb in Granados, waiting for a bus to El Chirol. After waiting for some time, you're hungry and you head to a nearby café. After supper, the two waitresses offer you a red rose plucked from a vase as you leave— perhaps a foreigner is seldom seen here. The girls lock up and fall asleep somewhere in the café, to work again tomorrow from morning to night.

The next morning, after a breakfast cooked by the rose-giving girls, you're off to Rabinal, Salamá, Cobán, and Lanquin. You imagine the birds singing on your private island. Upon arriving at a place called Semuc Champey, you find it is a rushing river interrupted over a thousand feet by a series of peaceful pools, each flowing into others below it, all in the colors of paradise.

You breaststroke slowly across the largest pool. You're now within arm's reach of your private island, swimming with fish of minimal dimensions. You find that your island is indeed covered with towering flowers. You float up to its edge and touch the living green crust attached to its entire perimeter, just above water level. The crust disintegrates as your fingers gently squeeze it. You discover that your island is too fragile for human hands. You never place a finger on it again.

You first sense sadness as the island fades from your grasp but are strangely exhilarated as it becomes the common treasure of all humanity, indeed of all nature. As you turn and swim away, a frenzied thought engulfs your head. "I will make a documentary video," you tell yourself. You reach shore and run for the hickory limb where you've hung your clothes and your pack. Your hand digs into the pack, pulling out the means to your new end. You plunk your Flip high-definition video camera the size of a cell phone on the top of your head, slap your cap over it tight, and make a mad dash back to the river. You need to return to the tree, however, to find something to dry off your hand later, when it's time to film. You grab a dirty sock from your shoe and stick that under your cap too.

Now you swim around nature's island and shoot the docudrama, thinking that you'll show your friends back home the island that's forever out of your grasp. You might even upload the four-minute production on YouTube.

The people who discovered Semuc Champey thousands of years ago asked themselves a pertinent question in a language that no longer exists. Why is there so much turbulent water just before the tranquil pools and a thousand feet downriver, but so little flowing through the pools themselves? Perhaps at the loss of life, they learned why: Rio Cahabón nosedives and forces itself through a cave for a thousand feet under the pools. It resurfaces a bit beyond the final pool.

Your island, and the several small waterfalls that drop from each pool into the next, and the spots where you jump, dive, or slide into each lower pool are thus above a deadly underground river. You decide not to make a docudrama called *My Private Underground River*. It's enough to know that, as for the island that was almost your own, a mad river runs under it.

Sure, on watching the video you did make, your friends will be astounded by the island's size. They'll see it's three feet in diameter. You'll have some explaining to do. To take your mind off the shellacking you'll get, you say, *I'M GOING TO FIND MY PRIVATE SAUNA!*

Voyage to My Private Sauna[11]

APRIL 17, 2010

Another strange river, you hear, runs deep in the heart of Guatemala. You don't know its name. If you can find it, relaxing at the river's edge will be the voyage's fulfillment.

You never figured you'd find it in a heartbeat, but you're on your way. Buses and microbuses travel on gravel roads from Semuc Champey to Tactic, Tamahú, and Tucuni, and on to El Estor to sleep. After a sunrise boat trip on Lake Izabel to watch a few of the 250 species of wondrous birds, there's another microbus ride and a kilometer's walk to the river of your dreams.

A pool many times the size of a Northern Minnesota sauna swirls in front of your eyes. Who could resist jumping in? Not me. Once in the pool, who could resist swimming into a cave visible only to those who explore?

A waterfall pours down the 25-foot-high stone cliffside above the cave. Although the cave is just five to ten feet deep and a couple feet from the water level to the ceiling, it's 25 feet wide fronting the river. The water inside is waist high. A curtain covering the entire breadth of the opening provides some privacy—the curtain made of 65 fast-moving rivulets, running like rain off a corrugated tin roof, all part of the waterfall. *You are behind a waterfall as well as in a cave!*

You hunch over because there's no room to stand straight up. The ceiling is rough shaped, like the skin of an extinct crocodile or dinosaur. It is dripping all over you, the drops coming right out of the rock. You realize the drips are hot! The waterfall curtaining off the river outside is hot too. The water inside the cave is very warm, and the cave is steamy. You're not only behind a waterfall as well as in a cave, you're in *your own private sauna!*

---

[11] A similar version of this story was published under the same title in *Kalevainen 2019*, ProPrint (Duluth, MN), p. 78.

Knowing that Finns don't have a name for this sauna, like they do for other types, you vow to ask your Finnish-speaking friends back home to give it a name, even if it takes you weeks to learn to pronounce it.

No one else is swimming in the river, a peek through the hot curtain tells you. After working up a sweat on the unsubmerged top half of your body, you walk through the rivulets to the outside pool, cooler because a placid river flows in day and night from another direction.

Picturing yourself as a scout for Lewis and Clark, you climb barefoot up the 25-foot cliff to the right of the waterfall, grabbing onto any number of exposed tree roots, all shaped like handles to help a tenderfoot. Once atop, you head for the stream running to the hot waterfall. Mindlessly you step into the stream, almost scalding your foot. Ouch!

You don't need to walk hundreds of feet to the spot where the *agua caliente* comes right out of the ground. You're satisfied with the end result: your private sauna. That's what you came to discover. So, you just sit on the ground for a long time, nursing your foot. Yours is likely the only injury today to be attributed to the earthquake fault line that runs from the Caribbean Sea clear across this country and into the Pacific Ocean. The Caribbean and North American tectonic plates are in a geologic duel, and today the victim is you!

You now climb back down the cliff and fix to make a video docudrama, *My Private Sauna*. It will be a hot sequel to the bittersweet end of *My Private Island*. You'll be the producer, director, and camera operator. You'll do the stunts for lack of any staff.

After hours in a van and pickup, followed by a boat down Rio Dulce River, you lay your head down to sleep in a town on the Caribbean Sea that has no roads leading in or out. It's called Livingston.

That night, you dream about arriving in Guatemala City the next evening, three-fourths of the way back across the country. You'll walk into a one-story hotel, Pensión Meza. You're determined to bed down in Room 21, which you can have to yourself for $7. Room 21 should be a museum, albeit tiny. Why a museum? In 1951, an adventurer lived in it for nine months before traveling to Mexico, meeting Fidel Castro, and later becoming the world's most enduring revolutionary war fighter. Room 21's occupant was Ernesto "Che" Guevara.

The very next night, you will produce a three-minute docudrama, *A Night in My Private Museum.* It'll feature just two characters—Che's spirit and you. If they give an academy award next year for shortest documentary film set in the smallest location and produced at midnight, figure yourself being handed the statuette by the titanic James Cameron.

• • •

In May 2010, after the blistering *Voyage to My Private Sauna,* I returned to Minnesota from Guatemala. Did I promptly implore my Finnish-American friends to name the Guatemala sauna? No, I confess I did not.

Eight years and seven months later, though, the promise came to fruition. It was worth the wait. Sitting for an exquisite evening with friends Eila Isaacson, Fran and Ken Lahti, and Sharon and Ken Panula, I recounted the story of my private sauna.

The fact that the sauna was still unnamed sprung into my mind. Did my friends respond to my plea to name it? Yes, I announce, they did! In minutes, Sharon and Eila fine-tuned the name as well as the spelling: *LÖYLY VESIPUTOUS SAUNA.* Next time I journey to the sauna sitting smack on the earthquake fault line, I'll carry a sign and hammer it into the nearby rocks. It will forevermore tell one and all that this is the *STEAMING WATERFALLS SAUNA!*

You must be wondering about the occasion for that December 2018 evening among Finnish-American friends. The six of us filled one of many tables in the historic Kaleva Hall in Virginia, Minnesota. The annual event was the Pikku Joulu (or Little Christmas) Program.

Discovering the extraordinary waterfall and the hidden cave (at bottom center).

Left: Hot rivulets cordon off the cave of surprises from the outside world.

The evening was filled with a sumptuous meal, a bilingual concert, and audience-performed Christmas songs in two languages.

My friends at the table not only named the sauna deep in the heart of Guatemala, they also participated in the program: equally memorable were the beautiful voice of Sharon Panula performing "Finlandia-hymni" by Jean Sibelius, accompanied on the piano by Fran Lahti; Finland-born Eila Isaacson reading in Finnish a centuries-old message of Christmas Peace (with the translation in English by Art Maki); and the chiming of bells in a "Traditional Christmas Proclamation of Peace" by Ken Panula. The mistress of ceremonies was Janet Eichholz.

The Kaleva Lodge and our Finnish heritage is a true gift to all of us, I tell my bilingual friends. To top it off, we live in a diverse society in a free nation and are showered with wisdom, customs, heritage, and the friendship of neighbors and acquaintances who hail from many other countries in our world. All are blessed.

The Fisherman and My Dog
THE YEAR 2008

Back in my shack town of San Pedro la Laguna, I swim from the volcanic boulders crunching on top of one another at the bottom of a cliff. In the distance, I see a fisherman in slow motion. He sits in a homemade canoe in the long reeds at the point. After pulling up two stones that act as fishnet weights, he paddles my way. The fisherman's name is Chema. He welcomes me to swim up and take a look at the pile of small fish he's pulled out of a 400-foot-long net that was strung below the surface since dawn. His bruised and faded battery-powered

A boy in his family canoe paddles on the bird-abundant Rio Dulce River that leads to Livingston on the Caribbean Sea.

Juan Alfonso Pop Xol, with versatility plus, moves from place to place in Livingston, his hometown on the sea.

radio is playing music. His cell phone is in his pocket. In a while, he'll paddle a mile to the beach where he leaves his canoe made of mountain cedar. He's not in a hurry.

To set his net, Chema wakes up at 5 a.m., an hour before daybreak. One day, once he was already out in the canoe, he realized it was only 2 a.m. He returned home to sleep until 5. "Why, Chema?" I ask.

"I was afraid."

"Of what?"

"At two in the morning," Chema answers, "spirits may be wandering on the lake."

Chema fishes some evenings, too, but not with a net, he tells me.

"With what, Chema?"

"My hands. I dive with a light and pull crabs off the rocks," he explains.

"Do you ever use a harpoon?" I ask.

"Yes, to spear fish."

"Do people fish with a line?"

"Yes, and that's what they did long ago. But you only catch fish one by one. I don't want one," he says. "Since you are asking, Tomás, I also fish with traps."

Chema talks quietly and is extremely low key. You have to keep quiet and pay attention to what he says or it might drift by below your radar. "I love the tranquil life of fishing," Chema tells me in Spanish more than once.

The next day, I see Chema on land. I didn't really know if he ever situated himself on *tierra firma*. "Let's go to Zoola's for a meal," I suggest. Since it takes Zoola's 75 minutes to prepare a meal—they aren't in a hurry either—we have time to talk. He seems fascinated by the conversation of the travelers sitting on the straw mat next to us.

"Where are they from, Chema?" I ask.

"From Guatemala City," he says.

He knows by their accent. I surmise everyone in Guatemala has an accent (particularly me).

Chema sees my digital camera and asks about it. One morning three years ago, when he walked up to his canoe at 5 a.m., he found a camera in it. A tourist might have taken his canoe out for a joy ride and dropped the camera. Chema looked at the photos. "Many showed a gringo smoking and drinking beer," Chema says, "and the guy in the photos never seemed relaxed." Chema used to leave the paddle in the canoe on the beach. Now he takes it with him.

"What about the camera, Chema?"

"I only had it two weeks when someone stole it," he tells me.

It was now time to call it a night, since one of us would be up before daybreak. "Thank you for the pizza," Chema says. "And thank you very much for the cuba libre, too. It seemed like you enjoyed your fish dinner, Tomás."

I'll probably see Chema a few more times. He'll be in his canoe, living *la vida tranquila*.

the year 2011

"The incredible rains raised the lake three meters and wiped out farmland," says Chema. "Now the currents around the lake's perimeter are stronger than ever, bringing up cold water from the depths. The fish I net have moved out into the quiet, sun-drenched center of the lake, too far away. I sometimes come up empty. I've had another job, too. I free-dive with a mask and snorkel down 30 feet to shove, push, and nudge the pilings for the new dock into place. The old dock got submerged. I work down there for one minute at a time. You've seen me come up shivering from the cold water. And take a look at these scratches on my body. I earn $6.50 a day. I'm finished going to that job!"

the year 2014

Chema paddled by again yesterday. The lake is even higher than before. "Are there currents in the lake nowadays?" I wonder.

"Yes, and they change direction frequently," he explains. "A surface current can go in a different direction than a subsurface current. They change in speed, too. A person who drowns is often never found. The lake is a thousand feet deep."

Chema also springs on me certain rules of the fishermen. He and three others have rights to a certain territory. Fourteen others have rights to a larger area. If a fisherman from another town puts a net in his sector, Chema can pull it into his canoe, paddle to the intruder's territory, and dump it on the shore.

the year 2015

Down at the lake, a beautiful golden dog jumps off boulders into the deep and swims by itself on several missions. I realize someone, who's just left, was throwing sticks into the lake for the dog to retrieve. A big orange now floats in front of me. After bobbing for the orange, the dog stabilizes it in its mouth and disappears. A few minutes later, it comes bounding over rocks to my boulder. It still has the orange and sets it on my rock, right next to me. I then toss a stick into the lake, or even two. The dog thinks two at a time are thrice the fun, I learn, and fetches both on the same swim.

After I leave and am high above, the dog is still down at the lake. It stares up at me for a long time. I stare back, motionless. I know what it is thinking—in Spanish or Tzutujil or broken English. "I'll come home with you. I'll be your best friend. We'll go swimming every day."

In the back of my mind: "'til death do us part."

days later . . .

I meet my future dog at the lake again. In secret, of course. I haven't found a way to make it divulge its name. I suspect, because of something left unsaid, that it currently has an owner. After my swim today, it rambunctiously knocks one of my sneakers off the boulder into the lake. It jumps in and fetches the . . . *stick* that was floating by. I had yelled "shoe" in both Spanish and English.

Within a few seconds, a canoeist paddles toward me. "Chema!" I shout. He is trolling, the line gripped between his teeth. He'll know if he gets a bite—hopefully his catch is not fast and furious. His canoe now approaches my rocks. He has something for me. "Wow, *gracias*, Chema. You found my shoe before it could sink a thousand feet. I've never climbed up the boulders half barefooted. And I won't have to today." A couple minutes later, he paddles toward his fishing waters.

The first years I talked to Chema, the passing fisherman, I never saw him on dry land. And then one day, as you know, there he was on the street. It took another few years before I learned Chema's full name. "It is," he told me, "Jose Maria Mardoqueo Cotuc Hernandez."

As for my dog, whose name I haven't yet learned, I'm still waiting to see it on the trail by my shack. When I do, I'll invite it in on a forever basis.

Finland Wins!

FEBRUARY 22, 2014

Hello Fellow Countrymen,

In case you haven't opened tomorrow's sports pages yet, Finland defeated the USA 5–0 in men's hockey, earning the 2014 Olympic bronze medal. Today at El Barrio's Saturday brunch buffet in my shack town, I'd found a seat by the projection screen. A 10-year-old girl and her eight-year-old brother soon joined me on the ringside bench to kill time while selling their mother's textile handicrafts.

They'd never seen a hockey game. "Is that ice?" the girl asked. I explained that hockey is something like soccer and screamed "g-o-o-o-l" when Finland scored yet again. "*Mira!*" (watch!), I'd say, so they'd realize a replay was coming up, slowing down the blazing speed of the Finnish shots. I asked the girl if she'd be able to explain to her *amigas* a little about hockey. She said she would, although it would be in her K'iche' language. Not to repeat myself, but FINLAND WON!

The girl wanted to know where I am from. I answered that my grandparents were from Finland, and my parents are from the United States. Today, I added, I'm rooting for the team from my grandparents' country. She had heard of it.

I could tell by the type of clothing the girl wore that the siblings weren't from this town. "Where are you from?" I inquired. They're from Santa Catarina Palopó—clear across the big lake. They'd taken a boat here this morning and would go home after, hopefully, selling some of the stock they walked around with. The girl wore her town's traditional skirt, made by her mother. The boy wore clothes that might be worn by nearly any boy in the world, but it looked like he'd been roughhousing in them for longer than most.

The two had come here by themselves. Their father was working as a mason on a house. Their mother was at home making handicrafts. I bought a small coin purse from the girl for $1.50. "How long did it take your mother to make it?" I asked. "Two hours," she replied. To me the purse displayed more work than could possibly be done in two hours—less time than the Olympic hockey game that, need I say it, FINLAND WON.

P.S. To my American countrymen, please excuse the ardor. I am still damn happy about that American Miracle on Ice in the 1980 Winter Olympics in Lake Placid, NY. The USA was the youngest team in the tournament, consisting entirely of amateur players. In a medal round, it played a professional-laden, heavily favored team that had won gold medals in six of the previous seven Olympics and was from its Cold War rival—the Soviet Union. The 4–3 American win was the top sports moment of the 20th century, declared *Sports Illustrated*.

Two days later, the USA went on to win the gold medal, defeating . . . ahem . . . Finland.

Ancestral Walks
FEBRUARY 25, 2014

"I feel Maya to the core," Mario of San Pedro la Laguna tells me. "In my mind and my heart, but most of all in my spirit." He says he has no Spanish blood, unlike many in Latin America who have some African, or Spanish, Portuguese, or other European ancestry. He speaks the local language of Tzutujil, one of 22 Mayan languages in Guatemala.

I now ask Mario if he feels he is (1) "Tzutujil Maya" or (2) "Maya" or (3) "Guatemalan." He is *Guatemalteco* (Guatemalan), he answers, and "all Guatemaltecos are Maya." In his mind, some of the "Ladinos," those with a significant amount of Spanish blood, are egotistical. The 22 different groups of Mayans in Guatemala, on the other hand, are like family to each other, he says.

Mario has told me over the years that he believes the Maya have *always* lived in Guatemala and did not migrate from Asia to the Americas via the Bering land bridge (a United States remnant of which is protected today by the Bering Land Bridge National Preserve). Mario said he is willing to temper his beliefs, though, if 21st-century science can prove otherwise. We agreed I'd buy a DNA kit for him from the National Geographic Society's Genographic Project. (National Geographic Society launched the project in 2005, with IBM as a lead collaborator.)

Last year, while at my shack, Mario swabbed the inside of his cheeks and sealed the two swabs in tubes. I carried the evidence to the US and mailed it to the project lab in Houston, Texas. The analysis should uncover the routes that his ancestors walked over the last 60,000 to 70,000 years. DNA leaves a long trail.

Will 21st-century science show that Mario's father's father's . . . father (and/or his mother's mother's . . . mother) was a Spaniard? Or that they migrated over the Bering land bridge from Asia 15,000 years ago? Or that they were "always here"? Specifically, where did Mario's ancestors live 5,000, 30,000, and 60,000 years ago?

The results are in. In fact, they are in my shack. Let's invite Mario over and take a hard look.

Everyone alive today either lives in Africa or they or their ancestors left Africa, we are told by the genographic report. Mario's direct matrilineal ancestors (mother's mother's mother to the nth degree) migrated out of Africa about 60,000 years ago. They left cousins to migrate to Turkey and much of Asia, including Japan and New Zealand.

Some thousands of years ago, Mario's direct matrilineal ancestors ventured across the land bridge from today's Siberia to today's Alaska. The land bridge was once hundreds of miles wide. Humans may have been migrating northerly toward that land mass from southern Siberia as early as 30,000 years ago, but they began to cross over to the Americas only about 16,000 years ago. Glaciers melted as the last ice age waned, and the land bridge disappeared under rising sea levels about 10,500 years ago. This route of human and animal migration—think mammoth, musk ox, and two-ounce lemming—thus closed.

Mario's direct patrilineal ancestors took a slightly different route. For the first 25,000 years or so after leaving Africa some 60,000 years ago, they were genetically closely related to my own patrilineal ancestors. Our lineage split in a region near Kashmir in today's Northern India and Pakistan. A few of Mario's ancestral cousins remained in Pakistan, while others migrated slowly to Scandinavia. His father's father's father to the nth degree, however, migrated to the Bering land mass and, perhaps 15,000 years ago, entered North America. His patrilineal ancestors were one of the earliest groups to arrive.

Mario's patrilineal side has left distant cousins throughout North America, and some help populate most places in South America today. About 5% to 22% of the Ojibwe male population in North America, including in Minnesota, share Mario's patrilineal lineage, as do similar percentages of Sioux and Cherokee males. About 27% of the Yanomami male population in the Amazonian rain forest does as well. Some members of Mario's patrilineal lineage wasted no time once they hit Alaska. They traveled to the far south of South America, perhaps in as short as one or two thousand years. Today, descendants of Mario's two lineages live in nearly every region of North, South, and Central America.

You may be just as curious as I was about how Mario would react to solid scientific evidence. Would he reject it, call it fake, take it with a grain of salt, accept it, or take weeks to consider it? I'll tell you the answer right now, because I saw it with my own eyes. *He embraces the evidence that 21st-century science has offered him.* He and his living relatives now know more about their ancestors than any relative from the 2,000 generations before them.

In the meantime, I'm wondering if a few of Mario's ancestors knew a few of mine in about 35,000 B.C., when our common lineage lived in South Asia on a lightly populated planet.[12] Did they speak the same language? Did they hunt together? Did they share knowledge about treating wounds, infections, and ailments? Did they tell true stories or tall tales?

Just how many indigenous people around the world have—like Mario in Guatemala—swabbed their DNA for the Genographic Project? Comparatively few, it appears. But National Geographic and IBM are about to embark on an ambitious project: collect DNA from 100,000 indigenous people in 10 centers around the world. "The project aims to discover the details of how various indigenous groups migrated from Africa to their current locations."[13] It's expected that much else will also be learned in this "moonshot of anthropology." Mario and many of us will stay tuned.

And please weigh in on the following: should I offer to take a DNA kit to a Kichwa-speaking family who lives 65 miles south of the equator in Ecuador? I may see them nearly every year until the 12,870-foot elevation of their Andean village plays havoc with my constitution. You may share your recommendation at TomsGlobe.com.

---

[12] The steps taken by my own matrilineal and patrilineal ancestors are retraced later in this book in "A Brief History of Traveling Genes."

[13] "'Genographic Project' to Track Human Migration," July 31, 2019, Bio-IT World.com, http://www.bio-itworld.com/BioIT_Article.aspx?id=44260.

BELIZE

A Convoy into the Past
MARCH 1, 2014

Last I mentioned to anyone as I jumped in the driver's seat of a Toyota 4Runner with 186,000 miles on it, I was planning to sleep in a tent, canoe into a deep cave, and join an army-escorted convoy to the Maya city of Caracol that has lain in ruins for a thousand years. Turned out the camping spot is closed, and I didn't have time before sundown to start exploring the cave where Maya artifacts rest on ledges, untouched. Instead, I swam for an hour in a cool pool brushed by a hot breeze outside the cave. The 4Runner later discovered Malfunction Junction, where each day a traveler or two rests on the veranda for a beverage— or for a couple hours. These hills are barely inhabited, the only alien movement a sleek ocelot prowling alongside a river.

Next day, a Belizian Army jeep did rear-guard our three-vehicle convoy for the last ten miles to Caracol. The reason? Four armed men held up 20 unguarded travelers at a river stop two years ago. The *banditos* fled with cash and cameras. Since they spoke just a few words of English and have never been found, Guatemalans were blamed. ("Guatemalans sneak over the border, cut medicinal plants Belize abounds in, and sell them in Guatemala," I was told.) After the safe passage to Caracol, I found myself atop Belize's tallest building, the Canaa Pyramid. Since I overheard a visiting couple tell someone it was snowing in Minnesota, I asked what the weather was like in Biwabik, Minnesota. ("It's snowbound," I was told.)

Over one billion other questions have likely been asked within a couple hundred feet of Canaa Pyramid, 95% of them between 500 B.C. and 950 A.D. In the 700s A.D., 150,000 Maya people lived in this mega city, far larger than any in Belize today. Will we ever know what any of the other billion questions were? What was asked in 850 A.D., when many Maya cities were starting to slump toward oblivion? Did a child ask her mother, "Why are we moving?"

The other day, looking over the shoulder of a university student studying near a cave, I noticed that her textbook was open to a chapter titled "Cause of the Collapse." She's majoring in Maya studies. It's now believed, she told me, that a 100-year drought that lasted through the 800s was the critical factor in the collapse of the cities. Thus, the mother in 850 A.D. may have told her daughter, "We're moving like many of our neighbors because we're suffering from the worst drought in human memory. We have to go now while your grandparents are still strong enough to walk. We'll find a better life and come back when we can."

They never came back, however. In 1937, Rosa Mai, a native logger searching for mahogany hardwood, stumbled on the overgrown ruins. Over the decades since, the pace of discovery and study of the Maya civilization of old has picked up. In 2018, for example, *National Geographic* reported on the revolutionary technology employed to study the rival city of Tikal in today's Guatemala, just 50 miles from Caracol and against whom Caracol fought historic wars.

This new technology known as LiDAR allowed scholars using aerial imaging to digitally remove the tree canopy. LiDAR "uncovered" about 60,000 previously unknown structures in the Tikal area. Revealed were ruins of a sprawling civilization that built a vast network of cities, fortifications, elevated highways, and complex irrigation and terrace systems. The population of the overall Maya lowland region may have been 10 to 15 million.

Central America, it's now believed, probably supported an advanced civilization that at its peak 1,200 years ago was "more comparable to sophisticated cultures such as ancient Greece or China than to the scattered and sparsely populated city states that ground-based research had long suggested."[14] As time marches on, new knowledge comes to the fore, just as it has for the last two million years of archaic human and Homo sapiens history. In some fields, like biology and astrophysics, the knowledge is truly "new." In archaeology, on the other hand, we are merely rediscovering some of the knowledge and wisdom possessed by millions of people in past centuries or millennia.

---

[14] Tom Clynes, "Exclusive: Laser Scans Reveal Maya 'Megalopolis' Below Guatemalan Jungle," National Geographic.com, February 1, 2018, https://www.nationalgeographic.com/news/2018/02/maya-laser-lidar-guatemala-pacunam/.

SOUTH AMERICA

ARGENTINA and CHILE

The Uttermost Part of the Earth

MARCH 6, 2005

Far greetings from the Uttermost Part of the Earth, as an old book title called this place. Now they simply call it the "southernmost city in the world"—Ushuaia, Argentina.

Leaving the ice and snow of Northern Minnesota two months ago, I headed south. The plane routes and highways end here. Ushuaia is on the southern edge of Tierra del Fuego, an island shared by Argentina and Chile on the Antarctic side of South America. Early Americans explored this area perhaps as early as 14,000 years ago. Rain, wind, and cold—the first whiff of March's autumn in the air—may have greeted them, just like they greeted me.

Travelers from several countries stay at my $7-a-night hostel. A Bostonian just arrived after bicycling 2,000 miles from Uruguay. He'll bike back north over 2,000 miles to Ecuador. According to the last world globe I saw, it looks like he'll be biking *up* all the way. Anyway, he takes no chances. To reduce traveling weight, he cuts most of the labels out of his clothing, he explains.

A world map here shows that Ushuaia is farther south than the southern tips of Africa, Australia, and New Zealand. Ever since I saw penguins play so happily at the Shedd Aquarium, Chicago's top attraction, I've wanted to be among them frolicking in the wild. And ever since I was in 100-degree-Fahrenheit weather up north in the middle of

South America, I've wanted to keep moving south until I could slide left and right off an ice shelf with families of them.

Loaded with travelers from Italy, Holland, and Japan, our boat made a beeline to an island of penguins—hundreds of them! The Magellanic penguins are starting a 250-mile swim north to a warmer region near the Strait of Magellan. "They don't like the cold," our guide says. When spring arrives in a few months, they'll swim 250 miles back to the same end of the same small island. Regrettably, to slide off ice shelves with penguins, I may have to visit a different island or continent someday. Perhaps the Antarctic Peninsula, 600 miles south.

Returning to the main island, we found biologists at the dock who had just rescued a lost King penguin. They'll take it to the island we just left and hope it makes its way home, which might be Antarctica. It may be a lonely swim, since there weren't any other Kings here today. And it'll also be an ice cold swim, I discovered by dipping my hand in briefly.

Visiting a museum in Ushuaia completes a line of Native peoples' museums I've explored since November, which started with the new one in Smithsonian-rich Washington, DC, and continued in Guatemala, Costa Rica, Columbia, Brazil, and Paraguay. The Yamano Indians near Ushuaia, I learned today, were nomadic mariners. They built a new tepee or hut every few days as they moved in search of seals, penguins, sea lions, dolphins, stranded whales, mollusks, birds, berries, mushrooms, and roots. They employed harpoons, daggers, bows and arrows, as well as slingshots. The Yamano built new beech bark canoes every year. They kept a fire burning in their canoe as they hunted or moved to the next nomadic stop. Once ashore, they'd use the embers to ignite a fire in their hut.

The Yamano children, sitting in the middle of the canoe, fed the fire and bailed water. The father harpooned edibles from the front while the mother paddled and guided from the back. Once at their destination, she'd leave everyone off, anchor the canoe out among floating plants, and swim ashore. Only women knew how to swim.

When Ferdinand Magellan "discovered" his strait, a natural passage between the Atlantic and Pacific, and sailed through in 1520, he observed so many fires he named the island *Tierra del Fuego*—Land of Fire. The fires died out when most of the indigenous people lost their lives to imported diseases, however. That was 100 to 150 years ago. For the 10,000 years before that, the Yagán and their predecessors had been the world's southernmost societies. Only one native speaker made it to the 21st century: Cristina Calderón, who with two relatives published a book, *Hai Kur Mamashu Chis (I Want to Tell You a Story)*.

I'll soon start my journey up north by zigzagging west and east through cracks in the Andes Mountains between Chile and Argentina. Meanwhile, if you are about to undertake an arduous journey, think about cutting the labels out of your clothing.

Scientific Americans at Work
MARCH 17, 2005

Do icebergs rain down on lakes during deer season? Do rivers go up steep mountains? I believe I can answer these questions as a Scientific American. Are you a Scientific American? All right! Come with me. And, if you're a Scientific Person from any of the other 194 countries in the world, you're most welcome too. (If you're one of the few who isn't a Scientific Person, you don't quite qualify to join this venture, though you're encouraged to read all about it.)

• • •

Let's break these questions down. Do icebergs rain down on anything? Do rivers go up mountainsides? Is there a deer hunting season here in the Andes Mountains that crush the border between Argentina and Chile?

Our job is to answer these questions and do it now. The coterie that we cobbled together includes you and me, Veronica (whom we're just getting to know), a geologist, and three others who may help accomplish our mission. We met each other on Tierra del Fuego, the island that was once stuck to the bottom of South America, which was once stuck to Africa, which—but we learned all this eons ago. Let's not digress.

We've made it across the vast sagebrush-like Patagonia of southern Argentina toward the Andes. Strangely set in this nearly deserted land is Lake Argentina. Yet people are not swimming. We scientifically reason it must be polluted. Turns out we've shot from the hip: we soon drink the lake water that flows untreated from the water taps in this town of Calafate.

We see the Santa Cruz River flow out of the lake toward the distant Atlantic, continuously trying to drain the lake dry. We conclude the lake is replenished by streams and rainwater. We're soon confronted with refuting information, however: rain is infrequent on this eastern side of the Andes, and only minor streams bring water into the lake. The geologist among us issues a challenge: "As the Scientific Persons we've professed to be, we must investigate and learn facts *before* concluding."

And so it is. We investigate why the lake doesn't drain out. We travel by road westerly from Calafate to the very far end of the lake, close to the Andes. Chagrined at our propensity to leap to conclusions, we've agreed to be taken there blindfolded. We're finally permitted to rest, left with only our senses of smell and hearing. We smell nothing, except fresh air. But we hear the cracking sound of rifle shots. It could be deer season. We also hear a quite familiar rumble. A thunderstorm must be approaching. We're treated, too, to a continuous sound of water flowing robustly. We're certainly near waterfalls. The combination of the three sounds seems weirdly orchestrated. A shot is fired at a deer, then thunder rumbles, overlaid by the sound of waterfalls.

One among us cannot keep a secret any longer—he's nudged the blindfold down around his ears and hears nothing but sees everything.

(Why is there always one cheat in a group of scientists?) "The colors are fantastic!" he blurts out. "White and wonderful shades of blue. A big piece of blue breaks and falls downward. It hits the water. Waves fan out, even whitecaps," he roars. These facts don't jibe with what we hear. "One chunk of the blue surges back up out of the lake, breaking the surface like a dolphin dancing in the air," he adds.

We rip off our blindfolds. We see fantastic colors and huge chunks of ice breaking and falling and floating and moving and surging. We see a glacier in the valley that runs far back into the rising Andes. As we hear what sounds like a rifle shot and thunder, we look a mile to our right. No shots, no storms, no waterfalls—just the rifle sound of the glacier's front breaking, and the thunderous crashing of the massive chunk on the lake's surface. Later, the same sounds and sights play out a mile to the left. Then they're right in front of us. Overlaying this are continual streams of melting ice running off the glacier, and the churning and heaving of the ice-laden lake.

This glacier, Perito Moreno, is nearly three miles wide, and all 15,000 feet of its front touch Lake Argentina. It rises 200 feet straight up from the lake's surface. Yet most of the glacier's front is under water, as are the minutes-old icebergs starting to drift east in the direction of Calafate, the Santa Cruz River, and the Atlantic. The bottom of the glacier rests at a depth of 400 to 500 feet on the lake's bottom. Perito Moreno is formed by two separate glaciers that join together. They begin 18 miles back in the Andes, close to Chile.

We ask and learn that the lake temperature is between 35 and 42 degrees Fahrenheit year round. We ask and thus learn that the fallen icebergs melt in a few days. We've discovered, as scientifically as we can, that people don't swim because the lake is too cold, and that the lake is replenished by falling and melting ice. It's indeed raining icebergs, although some scientists use fancy words like "glacier calving." And we've learned there is no deer hunting season, despite the sound of it. So we've answered some of our questions.

Rigorous scientific inquiry, the likes of which we do, comes with bonus discoveries. One is that Perito Moreno is one of the few glaciers in the world that's not receding, or melting back. I, for one, thought you could sit by a glacier for a thousand years without seeing or hearing anything. But what a little investigation will do! Perito Moreno is advancing at the rate of six feet a day, according to a renowned glaciologist. The glacier is also raining icebergs off its front at that same rate, so it's neither growing longer nor receding right now. We're also informed by local observers that some of the icebergs that surge up and break the surface of the lake are probably pieces that cracked off the glacier deep down in the lake.

We only have one more question to answer: do rivers go up mountainsides? We see nothing in Argentina to suggest a "yes" and feel smug in thinking "no!" But we nonetheless go over the mountain to see what we can see in the peaks and lakes and rivers of Chile's Torres del Paine National Park.

Our mountainous inquiry promises to be arduous. We pack as lightly as possible. We can choose from several trails, each miles long. We pick a route of two days of trekking, based on an estimated five-hour walk each day. The first day will be eight miles, the second seven. Most other visitors pick routes requiring three, five, or even seven days. They are from Japan, Australia, Chile, Argentina, England, Germany, the Netherlands, Spain, Israel, and Romania. Europe apparently discovered South America long ago.

We don't carry more than four ounces of water each. We cross a stream or river every half hour and drink from each and every one. Stopping for a long, tall drink also gives us time to size up the best way to make the crossing. The "five-hour" journey each day turns into seven or eight. We can't resist stopping at streams; lying on huge boulders that warm up by noon; sitting on logs and fences; and gazing at birds, lakes, clouds, and rolling stones. Every other trekker passes us up, sometimes noticing neither us nor the rolling stone, but making his or her contribution to the low average walking time.

Glaciers, lakes, and peaks 8,000 feet or higher grace the park. Most of the trails are surprisingly close to sea level, 600 to 1,500 feet. We don't rough it by camping, but stay in *refugios*, lodges that bunk six or more to a room—men, women, and strangers all together. (Those who arrive at Refugio Los Cuernos a little late, where they have bunks three high, shouldn't be surprised by which bunk they get.)

The first morning, we put our rain ponchos on over four layers of shirts and jackets. It's on and off with the poncho and some of the layers all day. Our trail runs for hours in between the mountains and Lake Skottsberg and then Lake Nordenskjold. The winds build to 50-mile-per-hour gusts. The gusts come in waves that last 20 seconds. Unprepared, we are nearly blown to the ground. We learn to crouch or sit in the nick of time.

The wind whips up Lake Skottsberg. We see nothing but a fierce white above it, exactly like a Minnesota blizzard whipping the snow across the road in front of the car. The jabs in our skin from the lake's water droplets are so sharp they feel burning hot.

True scientists like us must, nevertheless, work in what the geologist calls hellish conditions. Therefore, through gritted teeth, we observe. We observe a rainbow over every little blizzard on the lake. We observe where this lake-whipped precipitation lands. As luck would have it, most lands on the lush growth of trees near the shore—trees that we then conclude wouldn't even be there but for this phenomenon that we have the privilege of naming. And name it we will.

We look up in the sky—a good idea for scientists any day, but especially when you need guidance. The day-long clouds that have been masking the majestic snow-covered peaks break, but only halfway. Blue sky predominates to the right of the peaks, while the cloud cover stays in place to the left. A few clouds make it over the top from left to right. They are a lovely nimbocumulus as one of us identifies them, perhaps incorrectly. Another, who studied atmospherics and acting in college, dramatizes "Nimbo? Nimbo? Nimbocumulus?" A handful of the clouds now making it over the top start to roll. They look like a dreamy windmill slowly turning.

We now observe dozens of rock layers in the mountains parallel to the ground, slanted, almost vertical, or concave rounded as if South America's Paul Bunyan sat down for a rest. Dozens of layers, or hundreds? We stop counting at 55 because one among us—namely you—points to a river flowing down the nearly vertical mountainside.

"A funny thing happens on the river's way down," you inform us. "It starts to go back up." We remember the blizzardy storms that blow across the lake and water the lushy trees. Where does the wind go after that? The wind hits the side of the mountain and goes straight up, we notice. It's so powerful it turns the falling river into a rising spray. The river simply stops halfway down, and its water goes skyward until it's attracted to the mountainside's lushy trees. We excitedly discuss naming this phenomenon, too, as soon as we have time.

Near the end of our second day, we move a little faster because no one wants to sleep on the top bed of a three-high bunk another night. At long last, we arrive at our Refugio Las Torres and discover that its bunks are only two high. Also staying in our room are a couple from Seattle, as well as a young Spaniard and his Argentinian girlfriend, who met in a Yahoo chat room two years ago and are still in love. They sleep in a lower bunk together.

A debate begins. One of our roommates says that the daylight savings date is tonight and that we have to turn the clocks back an hour, making for a restfully longer night. I declare I know the rule: "Spring ahead, fall back. The month is March. It's spring. We must turn our clocks ahead an hour and suffer a shorter night." I have a winning horse and I'm riding it. After some confusion (partly because both Spanish and English are used in our debate), the man from Seattle blurts out: "It's not spring in the Southern Hemisphere; it's fall now." We all go to sleep happy, since we'll have that extra hour of sleep. (But winter's coming.)

The next morning, we, *Personas Scientificas,* end our journey, all hopping in a van that's leaving this great national park. We now know rivers can go up and icebergs can fall into lakes. A hemispheric conundrum tugs at us, though. Down in Tierra del Fuego, a guide on the way to the penguin island told us to eyeball valleys that have been deforested by beavers imported from Canada to create a beaver skin industry. It was discovered, belatedly, that beavers in Tierra del Fuego, unlike in Canada, have no natural predators, like bears. A Dutch traveler suggested that someone ambitious import North American bears. We almost concluded that North American bears would hibernate, like in the north, from November to March, which would be all summer here. They'd certainly die in a year or two from starvation.

You reminded us that, as accomplished scientists, we must investigate first. We no longer shoot from the hip. We agree that next year, we'll round up a handful of North American bears and haul them to Tierra del Fuego. Then we'll know.

Once back in Minnesota, I'll bear-grease my rusty old traps in anticipation of our mission next year.

Lug Nuts on the Loose
MARCH 12, 2005

You and I and our coterie of scientific persons thought our mission was over when we finished our trek in Chile's Torres del Paine National Park. But do we have news for our families, friends, coworkers, and bosses who expected us back long ago.

It was just a few days ago that we-the-blindfolded traveled to that living glacier, Perito Moreno in Argentina, and then journeyed to the national park in Chile. We were on our way out of the park. We counted up our scientific discoveries and talked about how our fellow scientists will be enamored of us for years—yes, decades!—to come. We were on a roll and discussed investigating our planet just a little longer. But only you and I voted "yes," and it looked like we were all going home.

A few loose lug nuts can change the course of history, though. You jumped out of the van first when the driver stopped to check why we were veering all over the road. You yelled, "The lug nuts are loose!" We all piled out. Two of the six on the back left wheel were missing. The other four were loose and about to spin off. After an hour, the driver managed to tighten three of them, and off we were. You and I convinced the others that this was a miracle of survival and meant we were supposed to continue our scientific mission.

And so it is. At a crossroads near the Chile-Argentina border, we find a new guide, Mariano. He may take us to a place where we'll make more waves with our innovative approaches to science.

"Let's put on our blindfolds!" you cry out. So, we do. On the way, Mariano, who's steering the four-wheel-drive gas-guzzler, marvels at the herds of sheep, the falcons, the black-necked swans preparing for their annual trip north to Peru and Bolivia, the pink flamingos that will soon fly to Alaska, and the dead skunk in the middle of the road. Mariano muses how one hectare of land in natural condition here could support 600 to 700 sheep, but the ranchers of yesteryear let the number swell, so that by 1928, there were a thousand per hectare. The land was devastated, and each hectare now supports six or seven.

You, Veronica, and I whisper that Mariano speaks Argentinian Spanish and knows the land well. He must be taking us through Argentina, not Chile, where we were just an hour ago. You say 600 or 1,000 sheep on one single hectare is a lot; maybe he means to say sheep per 100 hectares. Even though we're scientists, too, Veronica and I have no clue how big a hectare is. As with other unknowns, we might search the internet someday and be as smart as our resumes allege we are.

One of us asks Mariano if indigenous people ever inhabited the area outside our blindfolds. "Yes, the Aonikenk did," Mariano explains.

"The immigrating white man called them Tehuelche. The Aonikenk ate small blueberries called *calafates*, as well as apples the size of blueberries. And *yloylo* too, a yellow ball of fungus that hangs from trees that white men called Indian bread. The Aonikenk hunted the llama-related *guanacos*, the big Patagonian rabbit called *mara*, and the long-legged, long-necked flightless bird called *cheoque*. They used bows and arrows and sharp stones. They also wielded *boleadores*— three round stones each connected to a length of leather strap that, when thrown accurately, wrapped themselves around the legs of animals and white men.

"The Aonikenk never knew man could own land because it belonged to everyone," Mariano continues. "Wars thus broke out between the white man and the Aonikenk. The Aonikenk were exterminated. Nothing was left behind—not the Aonikenk, not the language, not their learnings or teachings. Only cave paintings and mummies."

We step out of Mariano's powerful vehicle—we all plan to buy one when we get home—and are led away blindfolded to a boat that takes us elsewhere. Veronica is designated by our new guide, liability-conscious Flavio, to help us avoid slips and falls. He therefore removes her blindfold. We walk for 20 minutes, then stop while Flavio attaches a strange and heavy belt around each of our waists. He straps a clunky metal apparatus to the bottom of each of our hiking boots, too. We then start off again, still blindfolded. When Veronica says "jump," we jump over the crevasses, she says. And do we ever stumble. But that's what some of us scientists do best.

We hike still farther, and now Veronica is gasping and possibly gaping at what she sees. "At least tell us about any land formations, soils, rivers, and rocks you see," the geoscientist among us pleads.

Veronica enraptures us: "Mountains rise up on both sides. At our eye level, running along the bottom of the mountain to our left, is a long peaked row of soil and stones that looks as if bulldozers have been at work for years. Along the bottom of the mountain to the right is an identical row. Closer to us, boulders, stones, and pebbles are strewn haphazardly as if on a moonscape. Streams flow everywhere in different directions. Small waterfalls. Sinkholes, too."

It's finally time to discover if we've been led down a primrose path. We sit down (on our gloves, Flavio insists). He takes our blindfolds off one by one, and with each, there's a whoop of amazement. We are back at our favorite spot on Planet Earth! But now we are out in the middle of our glacier, Perito Moreno. Sitting on top of 2,000 feet of ice. On our gloves, like Flavio insisted, or we'd freeze something off.

We see the color blue: streams crossing the hilly glacial surface, small waterfalls, and round sinkholes. Into the Andes, the glacier looms as far as our corrected eyesight can see. Running along the two sides of the glacier, at the base of the mountains, is a tall row of glacial moraine of gravel and dirt, neatly peaked, created by the glacier when it advanced, but it is now left exposed. Hither and thither are the crevasses we've been jumping over.

A surprise is about to arrive, but we don't notice his approach because we are harking back 12,500 years. In that Paleolithic year, a Paleo-Indian living in what's now Minnesota and Wisconsin would have seen the exact same phenomena we see if, if . . . that's where you come in since you're steeped in that era. You say the North American Paleo-Indians (or "ancient Indians") may have trekked over a glacier like this when: (a) chasing down a 14-foot-tall woolly mammoth that had tusks 12 feet long; (b) pursuing a pair of 1500-pound musk oxen onto the ice; (c) following the tracks of a 20-foot-long ground sloth that had claws 12 inches in length; (d) going after a deadly big cat with upper saber teeth 10 inches long; or (e) fancying the skin of a 480-pound beaver.

The kid in each of us surmises that Paleo-Indian youths may also have played a game of hide-and-seek down slippery slopes like these. We are about to test our theory that it would be hilarious fun to do it ourselves. I'm heading for a sinkhole. Veronica is lying down next to a stream. You seem intent on wedging yourself in a crevasse. Others are scattering farther afield. The geoguy is "it."

But just then guide Flavio announces the arrival of "the professor." We all stand up straight and clunk ahead together on our crampons. Today, we have a special treat, one no novice ice traveler has ever had before, going back as far as the Paleo-Indians. A learned expert has arrived. He's written articles for *Science* magazine and *Annals of Glaciology*. He is Pedro Svarka, Argentina's foremost glaciologist.

Jumping over a crevasse and clunking a couple minutes more, we arrive at Mr. Svarka's very mobile glacial station. He's about to get busy on a radio informing his land-based assistant that he's found the GPS transmitter he placed in the glacier last November. Next to the transmitter, a rod protrudes from the ice. Ten feet of the rod sticks out above the surface, and 40 feet is in the hole drilled in November. Mr. Svarka radios out that the transmitter and rod have moved a great distance toward Lake Argentina since he planted them. He confirms a finding of a prior visit that the glacier in this area is moving at about six feet a day. Later today, he'll look for the GPS satellite device on the glacial surface closer to the moraine near the mountains. He expects to confirm that the glacier is moving slower near the edges than out here in the middle of no-man's land.

Today a German TV crew is following Mr. Svarka. He stands before a sophisticated camera to explain his mission. I tell the assistant director that this glacier is the most amazing natural wonder I've seen anywhere in the world. She immediately orders a cameraman to aim his camera at me, sitting on my gloves. I repeat my story but add exclamation points, as we scientists do when speaking to popular media.

Now it's time to clank back toward land on our spiked crampons. We all get there safely. Flavio has not had to pull any of us out of a crevasse with a rope he'd throw down and we'd hook to our waist harness. Flavio would have been a good one to do it, since he's one of only four Argentineans accredited by an international mountain climbing organization (there are only 10 accreditees in the entire United States). Flavio prefers rock climbing to mountain climbing, though. He's climbed in many countries. His favorite spot is El Capitan in Yosemite National Park.

"Hold your horses!" the Wyoming-bred geoscientist now bellows. He's said very little on this trip, but all those geopeople are like that. We thought we'd walked off the edge of the glacier because we're now on gravel. Plants are growing out of it. The geoguy kicks at the ground like a horse hitched outside a Casper saloon. Lo and behold, just under the gravel is ice! Here the glacier is subterranean. The surface melts away little by little. A stony layer forms from the rocks that were frozen inside at different depths. The dark rock debris absorbs the sunrays and melts the ice more, furnishing water to nourish any plant that chooses to dine there.

We are about to debate names we could give this phenomenon when you interrupt with a plan. Next December, we'll haul truckloads of fine gravel onto a frozen Minnesota lake—Lake Ohbegon is your choice. We'll apply chemical fertilizer to the gravel and plant winter wheat. We may also plant rare arctic herbs we'll collect if we can swing a trip to Alaska. We'll find good lawyers in St. Paul and Washington who'll ease us over regulatory hurdles. We expect to harvest our crops about the time ice fishermen are removing their fish houses. You volunteer to write about our successful experiment for an agro-journal that's desperate for science writers.

"All aboard that's going aboard!" our guide Flavio screams from the dock. It's time for the short trip on the lake from glacial moraine to land. The captain orders Flavio to pull a chunk of glacial ice from the lake into the boat. As we motor over the lake at ten times the speed of the glacier, the captain's helper cracks the human head–sized chunk of ice with a blunt instrument, causing multiple fractures. A piece the size of an ice cube is dropped in a glass. Whiskey washes over it. It's handed to you.

Before anyone can say bottoms up, the whiskey's gone, and you hold the cup up to the bright midafternoon northern sun. You're admiring the thousand points of light apparent in the radiant cube. You then pull the cube from the cup and hold it up against the sun. "Dozens of diamonds!" we all exuberate. They can't be anything else.

You fantasize carrying this treasure to North America. They say glacial ice is so dense it takes forever to melt. We convince you to carry the diamond-studded cube in your mouth, where customs agents won't notice it. We'll divide up the diamonds later!

Just then, the cube squirts from your fingers into Lake Argentina. Our scientific mission thus ends without the prospect of instant wealth. We think ahead, undaunted. We agree to meet a thousand miles north at Lake Titicaca in August. We'll kick off Titicaca by officially naming the scientific discoveries we've made in Chile and Argentina: the blizzardy watering of lush trees, rivers that flow up, clouds that curl, and crops and rare plants that grow on glaciers and frozen lakes.

At Titicaca, we may also hatch a plan for another mission. Early money at Vegas says it will be the Arctic National Wildlife Refuge in Alaska. We could really do some damage there, the Sierra Club is already warning, since we've been spotted wandering around blindfolded while wearing crampons on another sensitive part of the globe.

But we do not despair. Your contact at the Environmental Protection Agency in Washington emailed you that when she walked by a smokedfilled room, Big Oil was saying they're searching for a group of professionals like us to monitor its activities in Alaska. On weekends and holidays, we'll be free to collect rare herbs and medicinal plants like Arnica alpina and Sitka spruce tips, as well as the bark and even roots of devil's club. As for herbs that are endangered . . . wait! We've already agreed never to mention that word.

Until then, remember another mutual pledge: "Don't take a trip with a bunch of loose lug nuts."

Atacama Desert
MARCH 27, 2005

How dry is the driest place in the world? The town of Antofagasta in Chile's Atacama Desert enjoys an annual rainfall averaging 0.07 inches. The town of Arica holds the world record for the longest dry streak, not having had a drop of rain for over 14 years in the early 20th century.

With Atacama's barely measurable number of water molecules in the atmosphere on any day or night of the year, wouldn't you think that some of the most farsighted astronomers of the 21st century would clamor to build "the most complex astronomical observatory" in the history of the world? And name it the Atacama Large Millimeter Array ("ALMA")? And in order to analyze potential life-bearing planets trillions of miles away, start building the Giant Magellan Telescope that'll capture images ten times sharper than the Hubble Space Telescope?

"Yes!" to these questions, *The New York Times* would report years after my visit.[15] Even if we are people in a hurry, let's pause to contemplate the fact that ALMA's 66 antennas give astrophysicists high-resolution access to cosmic action such as, in the words of a preeminent teacher of astrophysics in our corner of the Milky Way Galaxy, "the structure of collapsing gas clouds as they become nurseries from which stars are born."[16]

Not having a chance during my early 21st-century Atacama visit to check whether the chemical foundations of life on Earth also exist in distant galaxies (as ALMA would later find), I make my way to a miniscule 7,000-foot-high oasis in the middle of the desert—the town of San Pedro de Atacama. It's a town of dirt streets and mostly adobe

---

[15] "Destinations With Views That Are Out of This World," *New York Times,* November 18, 2018, p. TR1.

[16] Neil deGrasse Tyson, *Astrophysics for People in a Hurry* (New York: W.W. Norton & Company, 2017), p. 160.

buildings that absorb daytime sunrays and emit heat for people fast asleep during cold nights. And don't tell a native San Pedroano this is in the desert. No. "The desert" is reserved for the vast stretches of Atacama in every direction beyond the town's oasis.

I'll rent a bicycle today and travel back to La Valle de Muerte. A group of us ventured to that Valley of Death the other night under a full moon. Though the sky was filled with stars, they were all just in our Milky Way Galaxy and not in any of the 100 billion or more other galaxies. *Too far away!* And the multitude of stars visible above were only about one twenty-billionth of our galaxy's stars, by my calculations.

Let's stay tuned for the discoveries coming our way from ALMA and Atacama's Giant Magellan Telescope—and from other observatories from Antarctica to Hawaii, India to Puerto Rico, and the Canary Islands to Australia. In fact, after I've read the next paragraph and a few more that I can't close this book on, I'll search online for the newest incredible discoveries about our universe.

Meanwhile, still firmly affixed to Planet Earth, I buy a one-way ticket by four-wheel-drive vehicle to Uyuni in the Bolivia desert (oops, that's probably not in the desert either). The adventure will take three days. On the way, we should find geysers and lakes. Close to Uyuni, we'll find the biggest salt lake in the world. Forget to take sunglasses and you can't look at the brilliant white salt bed for even one second, I hear.

BOLIVIA

Mining Country
APRIL 8, 2005

I come from a mining family. I grew up a block from the Biwabik
Mine on the Mesabi Iron Range.

I thought I knew everything that stores in mining country sell.
As kids, we'd ride with our mom and dad to the town of Virginia for
a creamery can full of buttermilk, to Gilbert for blood sausage, and to
Aurora for seven-cent ice cream cones from Cherro's.

When I was old enough to play with matches, I walked to Neal Van
Soest's store on Main Street and bought a box of heavy stick matches
for nine cents. When I was old enough to smoke, a buddy clued me in
on how to steal a carton of Camels from the Co-op. When I was old
enough to drink, a high school student a grade behind me showed me
how to follow him into a local bar and order a cold one.

Now, years later, the small South American mining businesses I
see before me in Potosí tilt a different way.

This one sells Coke and Fanta, boots, shovels, and pickaxes. And
coca leaves by the half kilo, dynamite by the stick, black powder fuses
by the meter, ammonium nitrate by the bag, and detonators by the
dozen. I buy some of each—except for the boots, shovels, and pickaxes
—and toss them in my backpack.

I jump with others in a van. Up the twisting and turning streets
laid out in the 1500s we go. We stop at a working-class home and are
issued rubberized jackets and pants, rubber boots, and hard hats. And
we can't forget to grab a lamp that hooks onto the front of the hard
hat and a heavy battery pack that straps around the waist.

The loaded-up van now winds its way still higher. If we twist our heads around, we can see Potosí below, a city a little bigger than Duluth, Minnesota, and its 85,000 residents. Potosí is far south of our world's Mesabi Iron Range, where ever since we were little, we heard about the deadly mine jobs that confronted tens of thousands of European immigrants seeking a better life.

Like the Iron Range, Potosí (with emphasis on the last syllable— "SEE") is distant from centers of commerce and not on the way to anywhere urban. Unlike "the Range," however, Potosí is also far from lakes, trees, grains, berries, nuts, and wildlife.

Few people ever lived in this remote spot in the Andes Mountains until the Spanish came in search of riches. The indigenous people had known about a volcanic peak that points nicely to the sky and called it "Thunder" in the Quechua language. They also knew it contained precious minerals but used just small portions of the silver to make ritual objects. The Spanish named the pointed mountain Cerro Rico—rich hill, or mountain. Hundreds of other *cerros* rise up here, but only this cerro was so magnificently rich, the richest silver deposit in the world. This volcano-shaped hill is about the size of an average Minnesota lake at its base and three times higher than the Empire State Building.

Hundreds of thousands of miners—and maybe millions—died in the 1500s and 1600s at Cerro Rico, according to one study. They were mostly African and indigenous slaves. Potosí, one of the highest cities in the world at 13,420 feet, was bigger than London, Paris, or New York in the 1600s. It was the site of the Spanish colonial mint for centuries. Mule trains and llamas packed most of the silver to the Pacific Ocean. It was then shipped north to Panama, hauled by mule to the Caribbean, and carried to Spain by Spanish treasure fleets. The silver shipped out bankrolled the economy of Spain for 250 years and helped industrialize Europe.

By the time Bolivia became independent in 1825, the high-grade deposits of silver had been largely mined out. Today, the concentration of silver in the rocks is 4% to 5% rather than 85%. Miners, their wives, and children staged wage protests in the 1940s. The Bolivian army and police killed many. A few years later, the miners were authorized to form cooperatives and mine Cerro Rico themselves.

Today Cerro Rico has 120 active mines, all inside the mountain. Eight thousand miners toil here. The workers keep what the group produces, after a 12% government production tax. Tuberculosis and exposure to arsenic and lead take their toll, and many die before they turn 45. About 80% of Potosí's people live in extreme poverty.

Our guide Efrain worked in these mines for six years. His assistant Braulio toiled here for two years—until the day before yesterday. He's 17 years old and seems to be the one in a thousand who gets an offer to work outside the mines, although he'll be going back in with visitors like us every day. All the miners speak Quechua and Spanish; some speak Aymara, too.

Today I've joined a small group of travelers from Australia, Israel, the Czech Republic, Denmark, and Canada to visit La Candelaria Mine. The mine, about halfway up Cerro Rico, is a cooperative of 80 men. Some women work in mines these days, taking over the jobs their husbands had until their deaths.

Today is Friday, a good day to visit says guide Efrain, because many miners "drink on Saturday and play soccer on Sunday." "Turn on your lights!" Efrain yells. As we're about to walk in the mine's entry shaft, though, we're ordered to jump back. A railcar filled with rocks is emerging from the mountain on the narrow-gauge tracks. There's no warning blast from a locomotive whistle, for there's no locomotive. The ore car is instead pushed by two miners from deep inside Cerro Rico. Another car comes out too, pushed by two more men.

The miners don't eat inside the mine because it would make them sick. They do, however, chew coca leaves that keep their throats moist, lungs somewhat clear of the dust, and energy level high, they say. The raw leaf has none of the properties or sensations of cocaine, which uses the leaf as just one ingredient in a long manufacturing process also involving cement, gasoline, ammonia, sulfuric acid, and sodium permanganate.

Now that the two cars have been pushed out, we walk in. We're at 14,500 feet above sea level.

Within minutes, we're huffing and puffing, splashing in the water on the steel tracks, pulling up on a foot that gets wedged between a track and a rock, crouching down as the shaft gets lower, and when it's lower yet, crawling on our hands and knees, sweating, avoiding deep holes to a lower mine level, banging our hard-hatted heads on the volcanic shaft ceiling. I rise from a crawl to a crouch, but when my small backpack gets snagged on the ceiling, I fall to my hands and knees again and crawl.

One visitor needs to be led out. Another later asks if she can go too, but stays when told the toughest is over (although in three hours, we'll have to leave the same way we came in). The liability release we signed says that cave-ins are the most common cause of accidental deaths for miners. I'm wondering if, for visitors, it might be claustrophobia or sudden respiratory failure.

We take a break in a side cave where a life-sized statue of Tio is seated. The miners in every mine pay respects to Tio. Tio means uncle, but here in the underground mines, he is the pre-Inca deity who rules the underground underworld. Tio has the power to punish but also to help by preventing mining disasters and generating prosperity. The statue looks like the devil we've seen in drawings all our lives. This visual representation was created after the arrival of the Spanish and Catholicism.

We walk, squat, and crawl our way to the end of a shaft in the deepest part of La Candelaria. Vasilio, a 45-year-old shirtless miner, is pounding a rod into a one-foot-wide vein of silver, zinc, and lead. The vein is nearly vertical. He'll pound for four to eight hours to make a hole four feet deep—just right to comfortably hold a stick of dynamite and pebble-like ammonium nitrate. Day after day, miners will keep following this vein with the help of explosives.

Vasilio does not use a battery-powered lamp like each of us, but a powder fuel lamp that's lit with a match after wetting the powder with spit, urine, or soft drink. Efrain tells us a miner can hammer the rod in the dark. To prove it, he extinguishes Vasilio's powder lamp and tells us to turn off our lamps. We've never been anywhere so totally dark. With one hand, Vasilio repeatedly swings his short-handled sledgehammer, and every time we hear it hitting the end of the rod that's chiseling its way deeper into the vein of minerals.

Two other miners 15 feet away are pickaxing and shoveling dynamited rock into a railcar the size of my mother's old '58 Chevy sedan trunk. The miners do the work by hand and with simple tools. A jackhammer would cost $2,500, prohibitively expensive.

We give the miners what we brought from the local shop: a bottle of soda pop, a bag of coca leaves, two sticks of dynamite, two plastic fuses filled with black powder, two detonator caps, and two bags of ammonium nitrate (the substance used in the Oklahoma City bombing). In the afternoon, the miners will stick the detonator into the dynamite, hook it to a fuse, pack ammonium nitrate around the dynamite, and put the works in the hole Vasilio is spending hours creating. They'll light the fuse and will have two minutes to walk, creep, or crawl to a safe spot. In some mines, boys as young as nine light the fuse, since a child can more quickly get away through small shafts.

Tomorrow, the miners will have an additional ton of blasted rock to shovel into railcars and push out of the mountain. A dump truck will haul the rocks down the winding road where it'll empty the load just above a private company's processing plant. Boys will shovel the ore into wheelbarrows, push them 30 feet, and let the treasure slide down a hill to the crusher.

Arsenic and other chemicals mixed with water activate the minerals in the pulverized stone. The minerals rise in a foam to the top of slurry bins. Mechanical skimmers brush the foam through tubes to a holding tank. The foam dries, and presto, the remaining powdery substance of silver, zinc, and lead is shipped off to the USA, England, Holland, China, and other countries. Metal prices are determined every day in New York and London, and never by the miners' cooperatives, says Efrain.

That's what happens to the rock day after day after day.

But wait. We're still inside the mountain and our visit isn't over. We climb down rough-hewn ladders and short cliffs to a lower level of the seven-level mine. We see that other miners are shoveling rocks into a big bucket. The rocks are heavy beyond imagination, as we find out when we help out by shoveling them for a minute each. When full, winch operators—called *Los Wincheros*—raise the bucket with a mechanical winch to a higher level blessed with tracks. We give *Los Wincheros* and the shovelers pop, coca leaves, and all the fixings for another dynamite blast, just like the last group.

It's near the end of the workday, and we're all exhausted. Well, we visitors are exhausted just by all the walking, crawling, and squatting we've done—and working for one whole minute. It's time to break out the small bottle labeled "Alcohol Potable." It's seems to be the same as rubbing alcohol but 95% pure. One by one, the miners sprinkle a few drops of the alcohol on the mine floor, out of respect to Pachamama, the Inca deity who personifies Mother Earth. They then take a small swig and pass the bottle to those of us visitors who are willing to pay our respects to Pachamama and take a swig. "Don't sprinkle too many respects to Pachamama or she'll get drunk," jokes Efrain (and deprive us of well-deserved swigs as well).

Before the miners light the fuses, we visitors get going: walking, hunching, crouching, crawling, climbing, and sweating our way out of the mine the same way we came in, banging our hard hats against the low ceilings more times than we can remember, jumping back against a wide spot in the shaft when another car full of ore rushes by.

We too are chewing coca leaves to maintain our energy level at this 14,500-foot elevation. And we're coughing and cleaning our noses of a few million of the billions of dust particles we can see in the rays of our hard hat lamps. On our way out, we hear the explosions behind us. The miners follow us out of the deep and dark spot on earth where they've spent a big part of their lives ever since the age of nine or 11 or 13. We visitors may never again set foot in such a place, but they will, come next Monday.

Finally, we are out in blinding daylight. I peer into my backpack. I've spilled a couple dozen coca leaves. I'll be certain to give the pack a good scrubbing before I eventually go through US Immigration. But my mind has wandered, for I also discover a stick of dynamite, a black powder fuse, a detonator cap, and a bag of ammonium nitrate. I tell Braulio, who just stopped working in this mine two days ago to be trained as a guide-assistant. Braulio directs me to a miner. I wobble over and hand him the precious blasting materials, which may help the miners of La Candelaria earn their $5 a day next time they go in.

We've experienced a day in the life of Vasilio, the pick axers and shovelers, the car pushers, and *Los Wincheros*, who may live to age 45 or 50—if they don't get killed by cave-ins and explosions first.

Did we also just get a glimpse at the life of the old immigrant miners on Minnesota's Mesabi, Vermilion, and Cuyuna Ranges and in Colorado, Upper Michigan, West Virginia, and Pennsylvania?[17]

---

[17] "Mining Country" was published in a similar version as "Pickaxes, shovels, sledgehammers, and $5 a day," in *Hometown Focus* (Virginia, MN), January 25, 2013. "Braulio the Miner," below, was published in a similar version as "Braulio: A reluctant miner in Potosí, Bolivia," in *Hometown Focus,* February 1, 2013.

Braulio the Miner
NOVEMBER 15, 2007

Braulio was a machine-gunner in the army. But he is first, foremost, and still a miner. If he had lived in any earlier era beginning in 1545, when mines in Potosí opened, he would have been a miner then also.

Braulio would have worked 12-hour shifts. He would have emerged from the underground mine for his break every four months. His toil might have been made minimally more tolerable by the bountiful amounts of coca leaves the mine owners supplied to ease the burden and appalling conditions. Still, in the end, he would have been worked to death, one of as many as eight million miners and smelting mill workers who died for silver.

Back in 2005, some who knew Braulio were thrilled for him. He had an opportunity to leave mine work and become a guide for visitors from around the world who decided they could stomach three or four hours inside his mine. On April Fool's Day in 2005, I had made my way across the Atacama Desert in Chile. And across Uyuni in Bolivia—the biggest and highest salt lake in the world that looks like a frozen white Minnesota lake, except for a cacti-filled island in the middle. I ended up here in Potosí. I felt I could survive half a day in a mine. Braulio was one of my guides.

For weeks now, I've been on routes easier than those I followed in 2005. The day after I returned to Potosí, I checked at the downtown guide office to see if Braulio was working. He is no longer a guide, Pedro at the office said. Braulio returned to the mines because the price of minerals increased, and miners can now make a little more than the $5 a day they made in 2005.

Pedro then jumped up and walked out of the office, telling me to follow. He hailed a taxi. We eventually found Braulio's street, up close to Cerro Rico. We found one person walking on the desolate street. Who should it be but Braulio! He was not in the mine that day because it was the Day of the Dead. His uncle had died earlier in the year, so that night, the family would build an altar of flowers and food offerings in his memory.

Braulio seems like an old friend. He knows I come from the greatest iron mining region of North America. He knows my father died in a mine accident, and I know his father died last year—decades prematurely—after inhaling mine dust since youth.

Braulio now stuns me with a proposal: "Tomás, come to work in Porvenir Mine!" In a minute, I realize he is serious. I doubt I would have to fill out any form or pass a physical. And to work I will go! Braulio will instruct me on how to perform every task, except maybe how to light the dynamite and run. Don't expect many phone calls from me.

One question I do have, however, is this: "Braulio, how old is the oldest miner working at Cerro Rico?" Braulio believes he's about 55. "But why not 60?" I inquire. He explains that many miners are dead by the time they are 45. I step back, thinking about my future years.

We briefly move on from Braulio's decision to hire me to more about his life. His family was poor. He had to start work with his father at age 14. "Braulio, how did you feel the night before you went to work the first time?" I thought he'd express excitement, but answered, "I was nervous. My father told me how dangerous it is."

Braulio spoke no English during my first trip to Potosí two years ago but picked up many words working as a guide in the ensuing months. He hasn't spoken English since he went back to the mine but insists on using as much English as he can. He realizes, I think, that knowing English can be his ticket out of a short life span in the mines of Cerro Rico. Braulio may write many more chapters in his life. He's already penciled in the next chapter. After New Year's, he's quitting the mine and going back to work as a guide. Mine work is just too deadly.

I'm taking a rain check on Braulio's offer of a job. I'm sure it's transferrable, so if you'd like to work in a Bolivian underground mine at 14,500 feet, jump at the chance now. If you prove your mettle, they'll even teach you how to pack ammonium nitrate around a stick of dynamite, light the fuse, and run.

When you arrive in Potosí, ask for Braulio Cruz Soncko. Tell him I sent you. I promise to join you. Maybe in a few months.

The Second Daughter
NOVEMBER 11, 2007

Cochabamba, Bolivia

Imagine if you were the first daughter of a 16th- or 17th-century Spanish family living in the Bolivian area. A family made wealthy by the incredible silver mountain in Potosí or attendant businesses, or from the farms of Cochabamba that supplied food to those enslaved deep inside the deadly mines. You and your husband would live happily ever after.

Then you may find out, like I did, how the second daughter lived. Step with me into an imposing structure in Cochabamba, pay a dollar or two, and meet daughters of today. Gloria may take you around.

Experience the Convent of Santa Teresa, built in 1560. The first daughter of those wealthy families would marry. The second daughter may have come here, with the family paying a dowry of $100,000 in today's money, Gloria explains. A daughter as a nun in a Carmelite order like this lent great prestige to the family and likely won favors, too. But the parents, brothers, sisters, cousins, and best friends of the second daughter would never see her again. She was forever enclosed, never to set foot outside, not even in death. Families visited, but a heavy curtain hung between them and the nun. The second daughter was 14 years old when she arrived, unless all 21 spots were full. Then she'd wait until one of the 21 died and was laid to rest in the convent grounds.

The second daughters took a vow of poverty. Each had a room and a bed. When one family had a large gold-leaf altar built inside a vacant room so its daughter could pray more materially, the convent opened the room to all 21 nuns. At some point, all 21 decided they should not pray at the gold-leafed altar at all. This room was then locked up for 100 years, Gloria tells me. Many other nuns also spent their lives here but could not afford a dowry. Those nuns wore black, not white, and were servants of those who wore white.

Relief was provided, if relief it was considered, by the Vatican Council in the 1960s. Thenceforth, the nuns were allowed to walk on the streets and to see their families face-to-face. But no one from the outside world saw inside this grand convent until 2005—not even Gloria, who wondered as a girl what might be behind the walls.

The convent is still active today. And today you may visit and see nuns performing daily activities like sweeping the yard and garden. You may also go to mass any morning of the year. The church adjacent to the convent is a replacement but is hundreds of years old. Gloria explained that the original church was "through this door here, but it collapsed in 1570 during an earthquake." And through that door we did not go.

Up to the roof, though, we did go, where two ropes made of animal hide reach up and gong the church bells higher above. The ropes are 167 years old. They've rung the bells every morning since 1840. I was permitted to grip a rope and could've yanked it like others have done on each of the last 60,955 mornings. But it was seven minutes past noon. My clanging the bell at that hour would have been out of order—perhaps the first inappropriate act committed in the convent since it was built in 1560—so I refrain. But I will imagine until I die how heavenly my ringing the sacred bell would have sounded.

After the ropes, Gloria points to an antiquated medicine closet holding dozens of bottles that a nun acquired and dispensed periodically. "Is there *cocaina* in any bottle?" I ask. "No!" Gloria answers, but she does nearly touch one that contains coca leaves and another labeled "*opio*." I plead with her to open that bottle for us to inspect, but she politely declines. I ask her to just grab it so we can peer through the dusty exterior. She will not, but it appears to my untrained eye to be chock full of opium.

One may dream of peeking in a morning mass and listening as the 167-year-old ropes gong the bells. If you wander by well before the 7 a.m. mass, you may find the thick church door, dating from 1580, closed. The door may appear ajar, though, inviting you to give it a good hard push. That may be how the first parishioner gained entry on any given morning over the last several centuries, I theorize. But a good hard push that afternoon did not do it for me.

If you come to Cochabamba, pay a visit to the Convent of Santa Teresa. But if you yank on the ropes, grab a bottle from the medicine cabinet, and early the next morning give the church door a fervent shoulder or knee, don't mention my name.

THE COUNTRY MYSTERIOUS

Adventure Geography

MARCH 5, 2005

This is a puzzle and you've got 100 points already! Identify the country after getting the first hint and you get to keep all those points. But if you fail to name the country, alas, deduct 10 points after each hint. Ready?

Hint 1: If there's one thing we all learned in junior high that describes this country, you can blurt it out in one word.

Hint 2: A dictator ran the country for 35 years until the late 1980s. He's now in exile in the nearby country of Brazil. He wants to come home but isn't welcome. You can see his daughter's nice house from a main road in the capital. She doesn't have to work because they have lots of money.

Hint 3: The Jesuits arrived here in the 1600s. They founded many towns of about 3,000 inhabitants each, most of whom were indigenous people being hunted by slave traders. The Spanish crown exiled the Jesuits from the country in the 1700s. Towns like Trinidad and Jesus were thus abandoned.

Hint 4: If you take a taxi between the stone ruin towns of Trinidad and Jesus, you will drive on a hot, dusty road. You'll think the taxi driver is feverishly drinking an alcoholic or narcotic drink. He'll share it with the passengers whom he's picked up after you've made a deal with him for his taxi. If you ask the women passengers what the drink is, they'll hand it to you. You'll suck on a metal straw protruding from a wooden cup. It's filled with a mashed spinach-like vegetation. Your lips will go a little numb as you imagine a pleasant sensation. You learn later that it's the national herbal tea of this and neighboring countries. Nearly everyone you see has a cup and straw and a 1.5- or 2-liter plastic pitcher filled with water to replenish the cup when anyone, like a foreigner in a taxi, feverishly imbibes this "yerba mate."

Hint 5: One day long ago, the country's leader believed Brazil was threatening it. He declared war on Brazil. When another nearby country wouldn't permit our mystery country to traverse its territory to attack Brazil, said country declared war on that neighbor too. Still another country in the neighborhood joined in. Now it was one against three. The great majority of battle-age men in the instigating country died. The army then conscripted boys down to the age of 12, most of whom also died.

Hint 6: Did I say hot? It was 100 degrees every day (according to CNN en Español) but the local thermometers always said it was 110.

Hint 7: You go to this country because you wonder "What's there?" and then find out all these things, including the name of that dictator, Albert Stroessner.

Hint 8: Did I say you remember at least one thing from junior high? That one word that's fun to blurt out is "landlocked!"

Hint 9: You might get it mixed up with Uruguay, but Uruguay doesn't adjoin it. The country spelled backward is yaugarap, and forward it's "Paraguay." The triple alliance at war against it consisted of Brazil, Uruguay, and Argentina.

I wrote this puzzle because the country is still something of a puzzle to me—its history, traditions, current foreign relations, and economic disparity. Well, how many points did you end up with? If not many, then you're poor, just like that landlocked!, landlocked!!, landlocked!!! country.

BRAZIL

Glamorous Gals and Crazy Guys
FEBRUARY 20, 2005

Carnival in Rio de Janeiro! I don't know what to expect, and everything duly turns out to be unexpected. I do buy a ticket for one night in the grandstands of the Oscar Niemeyer–designed Sambadrome to watch a series of parades in which each samba group or "school" takes an hour or more to pass in front of tens of thousands of fans as well as judges, VIPs, and TV cameras. Each samba school has a couple thousand participants costumed up in the most colorful, flamboyant, and huge outfits the most creative part of the human brain can design. Somewhere in each parade is a band of 50 percussionists, along with a small group singing the school's theme song for the year. And don't miss each school's spectacular floats. When I leave at midnight for a street party, more people are arriving than leaving.

I visit two museums during my week in Rio to see what the most creative part of the brain designed 8,000 or 2,000 years ago, or just last year. But in museums, you see only planned creativity, for the most part. How about observing spontaneous creativity? Well, Carnival is the place.

Whenever I get lost, a celebration beckons right down the street. After being unable to wedge myself sideways into possibly the only bar in Rio showing the Super Bowl game (Philadelphia vs. New England), I head toward another bar but find myself at miles-long Ipanema Beach, adjacent to Copacabana Beach. As my Carnival fate has it,

I run into a party at Ipanema—six boys in a lively conversation in Portuguese with an old man who seems to be working. The boys then join hands and circle the man, dancing, laughing, and belting out a song.

A couple minutes later I notice the old man's job: collecting empty beer cans. My can is empty, so I drop it in his sack. Smiling broadly, he shakes my hand and speaks emphatically in Portuguese, an unknown to me. The six boys again join hands and now circle us men, dancing, laughing, and belting out a song. I'll never know what they were singing, but a couple of them practice their hundred words of English with me. They are teenagers and have been friends "forever." Each has a different skin color, one very light, one very dark, the others four shades in between. That beach party jumps the spontaneous creativity up a notch for me, with the other man and I as the subjects of sudden artwork.

Finally, Fat Tuesday arrives, the fifth and final day of Carnival. I hope I'll get back to my hostel by 10 p.m. and to bed hours early for a change. Just before doing so, however, I need to appreciate my third street party of the evening. No one pays attention to the live music. After one of the dozens of street vendors convinces me to buy a Skol beer, he offers me the only chair in the busy intersection. I am surrounded by hundreds of people and the most ornate, columned old buildings of Rio. Killing off that hiatus, I move down the street toward my bedtime goal but get shot on my legs, arms, face, and glasses with carioca—the shaving cream–like white foam that hundreds of celebrants spray from cans. That gets my attention, affording the sprayer time to convince me to buy a beer out of his cooler. This time the beer is "Antarctica."

With Antarctica now history, I can finally go get some sleep. I do notice, though, a group of 15 people who look stranger than most. A nine-year-old boy is dressed in boys' clothes, and three teenage girls and a woman are dressed in women's clothes. But so are the middle-aged man and the eight young men. The oldest one has chosen a flairy dance skirt. The younger ones prefer miniskirts and minimal tops with just a little padding, which give them very small breasts. I can't remember who says what to whom, but they are friendly and seem thirsty. I give one a bill worth less than $4 so they can buy some Coke or drinks of their choice. But in a New York minute, they tell me that we are all walking to the end of the block together, where drinks are cheaper.

Just who are these celebrants? A 15-year-old girl speaks some English. She is the somewhat nonessential translator for what turns out to be half an hour, oops I mean an hour, oops make that four hours. My companions are all from one neighborhood quite far out. The man in the dance skirt is there with his little boy and two teenage sons. Cousins Paulo and Antonio are there along with assorted neighbors. Paulo has sprayed small white breasts on his top and a small foam penis on the front of his miniskirt. Another carries an unclothed girl doll on the end of a string, the doll sporting a small foam penis. I wonder what Paulo will do if any of his appurtenances fall off, since he would look so incomplete. I find out soon enough. As the foam penis starts to come loose, the nine-year-old boy grabs it and hands it to Paulo, who erects it again on the front of his miniskirt.

Paulo and some of the others approach—I should say accost— any number of men and women. The accosters invite a kiss from the strangers, dance circles around them, make shockingly suggestive moves, and pat other men dressed as women on the fanny. Paulo is the most outrageous. He does all of this and, with a contortionist's body, dances snake-like around the strangers. He entices me and others to dance with him, and I am soon dancing the samba as groups of roving, singing celebrants and musicians pass by.

I wear an attractive but inexpensive necklace I bought at the Museum of Brazilian Indians. Paulo admires it. I am about to take it off and give it to him when he removes two bracelets from his wrist and places them on mine. I give him the Indian necklace. Next morning, I realize that both bracelets on my wrist are pink, which I'm sure looks great on any guy wearing a miniskirt and halter top, like Paulo was the night before.

Now, what are these people like in real life? The next day, Paulo and his cousin Antonio show up at my hostel, and we spend the afternoon hanging around Rio and taking in a movie. Each of them is 18, and each has a child and girlfriend, and they are to join the Brazilian army for a year that July. Since they only speak Portuguese and don't understand much Spanish, we barely manage to communicate.

And that's my story of barrio friends, including one Paulo, the craziest guy in Rio, on a gals' night out.

ASIA

2006 and 2010

JAPAN

A Favorite Country
OCTOBER 24, 2006

konnichi wa

I'm at the home of my 1970 friend Kimpei Ohara and his wife Mitsuko. After driving up mountain roads today, we ventured on a narrow-gauge railway through 41 tunnels and across 22 bridges up Japan's steepest gorge. At rail's end, feeling a burst of energy, I grabbed a hard hat off a nail in a wall and, since it seemed like the right thing to do, climbed over a barricade. I couldn't read the warnings posted at the beginning of the half-hour walk, but all's well that ends well, soaking in mountain hot springs.

Yesterday, we drove to the Noto Peninsula facing the Koreas across the Sea of Japan to visit Mrs. Matsuda, with whom I lived for five months in 1970–71. At 93, working a big garden, she picked fruits from her persimmons tree for us.

We've had dinners with Sato, who is director of cancer research at Kanazawa University, and Ogawa, a nuclear-weapons policy analyst for a government think tank.

When we first met in 1970, they were all students at Kanazawa University—except for Mrs. Matsuda, who at the time joined college students flooding the streets to demonstrate against Japan's use of nuclear power.

Kimpei's oldest son Ippo, whose fourth-grade class I sat in on during a visit years ago, is now getting married. Kimpei and his wife recently had a traditional first meeting with the fiancée's parents. They brought the customary five dried squids and large bottle of sake rice drink. Kimpei, speaking in a formal, traditional manner, asked the fiancée's parents to agree to the marriage, as is the custom. I understand that groom-to-be Ippo was wide-eyed, because he'd never heard his father speak like that. The girl's parents granted permission.

The two families, including other children, will meet again at the home of the fiancée for the Yuino ceremony, where they'll get to know each other better. Kimpei and his wife will bring several gifts, including offerings, for the home's Buddhist altar and Shinto shrine, if they have them. They'll first visit a special shop for advice on what to buy. In well over half of marriages nowadays, families water down these customs.

In 1970, I was taller than 99% of the Japanese. Now, quite a few men in the two younger generations are taller than me. Over the last thousand years, the height of Japanese people has ebbed and flowed a number of times in a wave-like pattern, I learned from a newspaper graph in 1970.

Today, in 2006, we ride super expressways and the rocket Shinkasen train that speed travel remarkably in this mountainous nation. Fewer rice paddies are cultivated. Fewer small stores and traditional Japanese coffee shops can be found. Starbucks and huge supermarkets lurk. Some youths go for creative dress and motorcycle cruises. Seniors who hit 100 receive 100,000 yen from their city. It used to be 1,000,000 yen (almost $9,000), but too many reach 100 now.

Kimpei is certainly much more a scholar of the English language than I am. It's his passion. He studied English intensely at Kanazawa University and, at the University of Pennsylvania, focused on linguistics, sociology, and history. Now an English professor at a Kanazawa university, he has often worked on English-Japanese dictionaries. He invited me today to a university English class he teaches. I snapped a picture of the 40 students after a request: "Raise your hand if you believe it was wrong for the United States to invade Iraq." Rather than counting the hands up, it was easier to count the one student who didn't

Shirakawa Village is reached at the end of a long ride into the mountains. Friends Kimpei and Mitsuko Ohara explain that Shirakawa developed a unique lifestyle and culture since it was snowbound every winter for generations. UNESCO has named it a World Heritage Site. A brilliant color photo may appear frequently on this book's website, TomsGlobe.com.

raise his—he told us he didn't have enough information. "What is your favorite country of all you've visited?" another student asked. That's almost an impossibly tough question, but as a guest teacher, I wanted to appear fast on my feet. "Japan, Guatemala, and Cuba," I answered.

But in a couple days I'll be in China. And then what?

After You Turn 90, Guess What!
OCTOBER 26, 2010

Four years after my last trip, I'm heading back to Japan. After flying 35,000 feet over Minnesota's iron mines, Winnipeg, lake-filled northern Canada, the snowy mountains 100 miles north of Anchorage, and the Aleutian Islands, Tokyo's clocks say it is 3 p.m. The sun never set on the jet since it lifted off from Chicago at noon US Central Time.

Parade participants in Tokyo celebrate their day.

On the ground, it turns dark and rainy. Clutching the umbrella I bought at a Tokyo train station, I hunt for the tatami-matted ryokan I reserved. I finally step into an actual hotel to ask. A worker comes out in the rain with his umbrella, and we slosh through the streets for blocks. I can't thank the man from the competitor lodging enough, but he is happy to help me. People smile and laugh so much in Japan!

On this trip, I have to hit Nara, a city celebrating its anniversary as the nation's first capital. Nara enjoyed that distinction for only a few decades, and no one actually remembers those days, which started in 710. Kyoto was next as the capital—until 1868—and there I find a castle, Buddhist temples, exquisite gardens, and a desolate path up through the mountains to a Shinto shrine by the smallest of waterfalls. As with my visit four years ago in 2006, many words I hear seem familiar, bringing me back to those winter months in 1970–71 after college. That's when I lived in an old samurai house with Mr. and

Mrs. Matsuda in Kanazawa, studying Japanese using reel-to-reel tapes recorded by my friend Kimpei.

Another good friend from the University of Kanazawa, where I whiled away time in 1970, is Ogawa. I journeyed to his hometown on a local mountain train on a snowy New Year's Day in 1971. His family first ushered me to a traditional Japanese *ofuro* wooden soaking tub of steaming water. Offering the *ofuro* is a customary and incredibly warm welcome. Over dinner, his father and I talked about his service as a soldier in the Pacific Theater of World War II.

A few years after my New Year's visit, Ogawa earned a PhD from Yale University and would work for many years in Tokyo as a Defense Ministry think tank analyst on nuclear weapons. Now in 2010, he invites me to return to his childhood village. His mother lives alone in a big house in the village. She is 84.

On this visit, she draws figures of her childhood for me on a scrap of paper. One drawing shows her wearing a raincoat made of rice stalks. Her school was an hour's walk away. I inquire if the difference in the dialects and accents of Japan have diminished in her lifetime. "Yes," mother and son answer, due first to radio, then TV and travel. They comment on the distinctive dialect in their area.

"Mrs. Ogawa, did you hear American planes fly over your village during the war?"

"Yes, in the night the bombers were on their way to the city of Toyama," she remembers. "We turned off our town's lights. We could see red in the sky over the mountains toward Toyama after the bombing."

Mrs. Ogawa serves us eight kinds of raw fish, bamboo shoots that grow wild near town, mushrooms, vegetables, and later a wine she made from grape-sized jujube fruits. We keep snacking. One delicacy is a minnow-sized fried fish called *ayu*, or sweetfish. I am flummoxed about whether you're supposed to eat the head, backbone, and tail fin. I watch Ogawa. He eats them hook, line, and sinker. I follow suit.

The next day, I am again at the home of my 1970 friend Kimpei and his wife. Kimpei sometimes refers to Zen Buddhism philosophy, saying, *"One day is a life. At the end of the day, you should be satisfied with what you've done as if it were your life."*

Kimpei inquires whether we can use the phrase "forest bath" to refer to the wonderful feeling you experience when you find yourself walking in a tranquil forest. Upon contemplation, I answer that I, for one, feel you could use that description—not mentioning that I (for one) have sometimes felt I *was a tree* in a prior life.

A dozen years later, I read that Japan has exported "its balm for battered souls: *shinrin-yoku*, or forest bathing." A trio of books arrived on North American shores, each with the phrase "Forest Bathing" in its title.[18] One suggests (according to Reviewer Browning) that we "[s]tring a hammock between cedars. Better yet, sprawl on the moss and let the weight of your body sink into the earth"—helpful for blood pressure, blood-sugar levels, and stress. Another instructs us to "count the various shades of green," reminding me that I counted 11 different colors of flowers as I sat on the veranda at my favorite hangout in Columbia, Reserva El Cairo. I'd suggest you intensify these benefits with a soothing visit to the moss gardens designed in 1562 at Obai-in Temple, a secret subtemple of Daitoku-ji Temple in Kyoto, Japan. Or, in a forest near you, look for some of the 17,000 known species of lichens, an organism with a mind all its own that's neither plant nor animal.

• • •

Straining your lower back! If you do it, then do it in Japan, I conclude. What a pain it was as I traveled in Nara, Kyoto, and Kanazawa. Kimpei and his wife Mitsuko advise that we must make an appointment first thing in the morning with a mother and daughter team that practices the Japanese folk treatment Ryojutsu. You are warned on the 10-minute drive that patients might plead, "Stop! Stop!" to no avail.

---

[18] Dominique Browning, "Japanese Forest Bathing Gives Tree-Hugging a Whole New Dimension," *New York Times Book Review,* December 2, 2018, p. 58.

"Lie down on your stomach on the tatami mat," I am told. The
pain begins right away. The daughter pulls on my toes, one by one.
Too bad I have 10 in all. The big toes are the worst. "Don't pull my big
toes out of their sockets!" I want to yell over and over. "God put them
in there for a reason!" They return to my toes several times over the
next hour, but thankfully, I have shoulder, back, and waist muscles
that also need to be worked over or stepped on with force.

"You eat a lot of vegetables," the mother tells me as Kimpei trans-
lates. "Your body is strong, but you have a heart that pumps weakly.
Stop taking the ibuprofen painkiller you bought at the pharmacy. Avoid
cold drinks and coffee. We'll show you exercises to do."

I stand up. My back feels much improved. By the third day, it's
85% better. It seems like a miracle. No wonder the Japanese live well
into old age. *Why not entice the mother and daughter to set up shop
in the US?* I'm thinking. *It'll cost $35 for the hour. Patients will be
forewarned that they'll never again forget they've got 10 toes.*

By Sunday, I am spry. We drive to visit Mrs. Masuda at a nursing
home. She'll be 98 in January. For years I've called Mrs. Matsuda "my
Japanese mother." I lived at her house free for five months in 1970.
I've visited her several times since, once with my real mom in the 1980s.
More recently, a young Chinese woman came under Mrs. Matsuda's
guidance. She went with us Sunday. Mrs. Matsuda's friends know she
has an American son and a Chinese daughter. So I have a Chinese
sister, I'm happy to report.

Mr. Matsuda, who was always busy testing chemicals in the lab he'd
set up in the house built for samurai, died in the 1980s. Mrs. Matsuda
later moved from Kanazawa to the rural Noto Peninsula and lived
there until this year. For her private room in the nursing home and all
food and other costs, the charge is about $1,500 a month. As a young
woman in her 20s, she overcame tuberculosis with traditional healing
when nothing else worked. As a university student in the 1930s, she
demonstrated against Japan's invasions of other Asian countries. Her
courage put her in prison for two winters. When I lived at her house

in 1970–71, she was still carrying her convictions into the streets, joining students protesting nuclear power plants. Later, while in her 70s, she was a major force in organizing women's cooperatives in Kanazawa.

She told me once about her imprisonment. The first time, the police knocked on her door and ordered her to leave with them. She didn't know she would be jailed for the winter. She didn't have enough blankets. She had no books. The second year, she made the police wait as she gathered necessities. She was thus imprisoned for another winter, as were some of her like-minded fellow university students. I realized we can learn history—even Asian history—by talking to people who've lived it.

Now it is 2010. Mrs. Matsuda, 97, has become best friends with an 88-year-old nursing home resident. On Sunday, when we visited, Mrs. Matsuda spoke these words of wisdom: "Try to live a long time. You can have many friends. *And you never know who you'll meet after you turn 90.*"

CHINA

Goodbye, Lee Tung
NOVEMBER 1, 2006

Hong Kong. In the city of gleaming high-rise towers and the ultimate subway system, I find a busy side street that perhaps hasn't changed much in decades. Inside a tiny convenience store, I count eight metal pots using up all the counter space. The cover on each pot is many-dented. "Soup," I order, and am asked if I like Filipino food. Now I recognize the Tagalog language spoken by the other customers and soon am served a vegetable stew and a bowl of rice covered with spicy chunks of meat.

The best-selling items at this store are telephone cards and Benson & Hedges cigarettes. The owner doesn't have to stand up or even reach for them. He has them in a handy drawer. A man speaking quietly on his cell phone on the street suddenly screams into it. He now runs alongside the store still screaming angry words. I ask the owner what he's saying. I don't get an answer.

A few steps away, a vendor is peddling other foods. An English-speaking customer helps me out. I soon have a soy pastry bar and a cup of tofu chunks in hot water. The customer explains that I am supposed to open the ziplock bag of brown sugar I'm being given and sprinkle it on the tofu. I walk away with that in mind.

Down a few blocks, I feel compelled to sprinkle the brown sugar. Just then, I spy an eerily quiet side street. Turning onto it to prepare my tofu, I sense isolation, loss, and sadness. Dozens of six-story tenement buildings line both sides of the winding street all the way to the end.

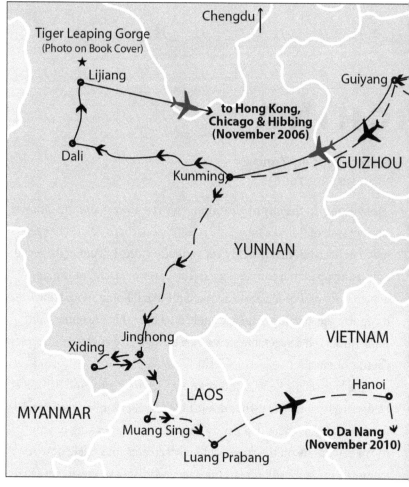

Storefronts occupy every ground floor. Every store is abandoned, every tenement empty.

The same sign is posted on all buildings: "This Is an Urban Renewal Authority Property." Doors are padlocked. Letters getting dirtier by the week are jammed in mail slots. The business signs reveal the recent past—Chuen Fat Printing Company, Graley Company Shirtmakers, Dr. Ho Sai Kwan, and all the others.

It's a quiet place to eat my tofu. But I then spot Starbucks in a new building past the intersection. I grab from my backpack the paper cup I saved from a visit to another Starbucks yesterday, in case

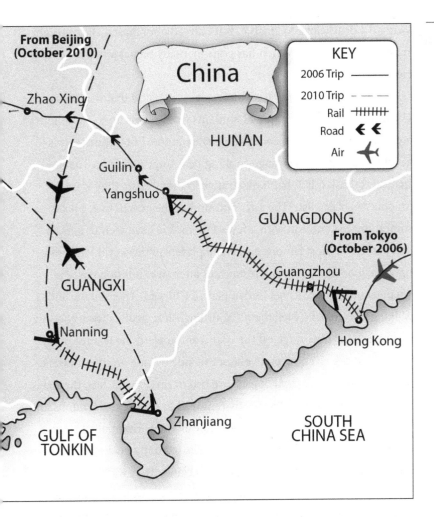

of an emergency. I pour in the tofu, sprinkle the brown sugar, affix the cover, jump on the escalator, and sit inside Starbucks for free, slurping tofu, looking out the window at the desolate urban renewal street. Now I notice the sign: Lee Tung Street.

• • •

A modern train zips from Hong Kong to Guangzhou, which when I was in grade school—and for centuries' worth of our ancestors—used to be Canton. The 100th Canton Export Commodities Fair is in full swing. I'd dearly love to crash it, but I already purchased an overnight train ticket to Guilin, which has gone by many names since the centuries B.C.

During a quick foray to Shamian, a river island in downtown Canton (oops, Guangzhou), 11 students from towns up to eight hours away who are attending college here stare at me. I first think this is because I am eating a strange-looking pear imported from Thailand. Instead, I think it is I that look strange to them. Also, they want to practice their English. The girls outnumber the guy 10 to 1. I have something in common with a few of them. We have seen in person one of the two most famous basketball players in the world. They saw national icon Yao Ming at a restaurant after an exhibition game in Guangzhou. I saw Michael Jordan play in Chicago. After talking and walking a few blocks, I tell them, "Your English is great!" I wave goodbye and search for the bridge off the island and toward the train station.

Across the river, several vendors sit side by side on the sidewalk. Set on the ground in front of each are two or three tigers' feet, the claws nicely cleaned and the skin neatly removed to expose dry tendons and veins. I inquire whether a photo would be all right. They politely refuse, even though I show them some yuan bills from my pocket. They not only have whole feet but also individual claws. They want me to buy at least one claw into which I could drill a hole—wouldn't I be happy with the specimen dangling from a chain on my belt? I decline. The claw looks like it would cut deep into flesh. Later, I'd conclude that the trade in tiger feet is illegal, and a picture would shred every seller's legal defense. (And who knows what international organization I might send the photo to, if I were that kind of person.)

I leave the tigers' claws behind and squeeze into a taxi. I'm late to the train station because of the horrific Saturday (is a workday) rush-hour traffic. When I find the right counter quite by accident (much happens quite by accident), I learn that my ticket is worthless because I'm late. I shell out another 207 yuan ($26) for a "soft sleeper" leaving soon for Guilin. I push my way through the station along with hundreds of others about to board the train. Some will get off along the way, since they're heading to the Chinese hinterlands.

I'm in a soft sleeper by 10 p.m. Mine is a middle bunk in a six-berth car. It's the exercise I got at the Mesabi Family YMCA that enables me to contort my way up there. Below are a crying baby and his mother. Across, a man snores off and on all night. It's a far cry from my Hong Kong hotel three nights earlier: the small dorm room bunked guys from the world-class cities of Paris, Manila, Helsinki, Berlin, and Biwabik.

My roommates get off the train at 6 a.m. I'm in Guilin at 10. I find myself negotiating with a guide to visit the city's park and cave highlights from 11 to 3. We wheel and deal using his 20-word English vocabulary and our apparent understandings. He pays for the taxis from place to place out of the 20 yuan—or $2.50—I'll give him at the end of our day. At noon, we're at the second park. He leads me to a cave entrance. I'm to meet him back at the entrance when I get out. The cave leader guides my group through stupendous caverns sporting pools, underground waterfalls, stalagmites, and those that point the other way around.

We exit the cave quite a distance from the entrance. When I finally find my way back, my guide is gone. I could tell earlier that he was unfamiliar with this cave—and perhaps its ins and outs. I hope he didn't slip into the cave looking for me and get pierced by a stalagmite.

On the street, I ponder. A kid is sitting on an old motorcycle. He has two overly worn helmets. He looks at me several times but says nothing. I start to wonder if he's in the ride business. I finally say "taxi?" and he somehow affirms. We write our cost offers and counteroffers on my city map, thus obliterating the sites I once planned to see. I pay him six yuan for a ride to the train station so I can grab my backpack and make my way to the famous little city of Yangshuo.

I don't notice that the kid has wrapped a towel tight around his engine. We take off. Within a mile, the motorcycle dies. I point to the gas tank with a question mark. He points to the towel with a period, so I know our trip together is over. The towel hasn't stopped the leak. Before I can motion "what now?" with my hands, he shouts out, seemingly by name, to a moving motorcyclist. Cool that he happens to know the next person going by in this city of 1.3 million, I think. But perhaps not. He just hands my new driver some of the six yuan I've paid, and off I go with my new driver. That's how I get to the train station for a bus ride to Yangshuo.

And that's how I spent 26 yuan—$3.30—on my day in Guilin. I (or any visitor) could go to Guilin a hundred times and never repeat that experience. Just by chance and happenstance do we have a particular peculiar experience, perhaps never to be replicated by anyone.

And that's also how a billion days go every day for the world's inhabitants. Novelists, filmmakers, and playwrights do take valiant stabs at turning some of our trillions of special experiences into stories. Many have been related orally and in writing over the millennia. The oldest story ever written is thought to be "The Epic of Gilgamesh"—who was two parts god and one part man. The tale was written on clay tablets in Sumer over four thousand years ago. The story of my day in Guilin may not survive that long. But now that it's on the page, its life span has just been extended beyond the confines of my own memory.

• • •

Yangshuo is home to sharp limestone karst pinnacles that rise skyward from the rice-producing fields amid rivers and streams winding toward the Yangtze River. Or is it the Yellow or the Pearl River? I arrange a river ride on a narrow bamboo raft. The oarsman speaks no English. He pushes and steers the raft with a bamboo pole while bantering off and on for three hours with fishermen on similar lengthy rafts.

Farmers near the river have cut their rice and tied hundreds of bundles to dry. They're starting to stick the bundles head first into threshing machines that knock the grain off in 6 to 12 seconds. The

A bamboo raft ride in Yangshuo devours hours, but we have a break at a bridge built in 1412.

machines, shaped like a covered baby stroller, are run by foot power applied to a paddle wheel. All make the same churning sound, heard for hundreds of feet. They were built at least a century ago, I hear from a Chinese who might be surmising.

On the raft trip I learn the Chinese words for "Sit down!"—I think. As we approach a low bridge, just after the one built in 1412, the oarsman gives me a card. I stand up and hand it to the toll taker who's up on the bridge making sure he gets paid by rafts passing underneath. He grabs the card from me while barking, *zuo xia*! I conclude these two sharp words have to mean "sit down!" I suppose he's seen people get knocked into the river as their raft floats under the low stone bridge. I'm wondering if Nixon, Carter, the first Bush, Clinton, and the top Chinese leaders, who've all visited the rivers of Yangshuo, got the same *zuo xia*! warning. I can think of some who perhaps suffered concussions right at this historic spot.

• • •

Before I fall asleep in the hills of Yangshuo, a few of many question marks stare me in the mind's eye. How did the people who were forced to abandon Lee Tung Street in Hong Kong feel as they were leaving? How did the tenement dwellers, Dr. Ho Sai Kwan, the workers at the printing company, and the shirt makers say goodbye to their street? And Lee Tung, were you a real person? And is there any way you felt the thousand farewells?

• • •

I did not immediately look for the answers to these questions, since at the time, searches were old world. I did, however, search a dozen years later. The 2007 demolition of Lee Tung Street was "seen by many as causing irreparable harm to the cultural heritage of Hong Kong," reports Wikipedia. I learn that hundreds of thousands of people shopped on that street for wedding cards, name cards, and traditional calendars. The numerous family businesses built through generations were forced to relocate to much less viable areas. A grassroots citizens' group made counterproposals to the master plan for urban renewal without success.

The place is now a luxury shopping and housing development.

Goodbye, Lee Tung. But who were you? And did you hear several hundred thousand farewells?

The Pitch-Black Barn and Turnip Ice Creams
NOVEMBER 10, 2006

A week after I bid my own farewell to Lee Tung and Hong Kong, I race by van, bus, foot, plane, and taxi to Kunming via Guiyang. There, I find a former Holiday Inn hotel that carries CNN and BBC—the better channels to watch the US midterm election results, due to start trickling in the next day at 8 a.m. China time, when the polls close in the US East.

Guiyang and Kunming are cultural shocks after five days and nights in mountain villages where people speak Yao, Dong, or Miao. Some villages were settled 700 years ago during the Ming Dynasty, when Mongols in the north pushed the Han Chinese south. Many ethnic groups then migrated into the mountains.

On the van ride out of Miao-speaking Longde (long-DAY), an English teacher tells me he left the village at a young age to attend

Stopping for a night's rest in an ethnic village during days of travel between Yangshuo and Guiyang.

school. Learning Chinese was harder than learning English later, he says. I don't know Miao or Chinese, of course, but the evening before when I walked into Longde, a woman approached me. She put her clasped hands against her ear and tilted her head. I guessed that meant sleep. I gestured affirmatively and thus had an upstairs bed in the building set aside for travelers (toilet across the street, sink on the street).

Long bus rides over treacherous roads are the order of the week, catching two-second glimpses through the bus windows—a man smoking on a motorcycle with a side of beef slung over the back of his bike, waterwheels churning in rivers bringing water to rice fields peopled by workers, a woman carrying a heavy basket load at each end of a flexible pole carried on her shoulder. I catch a one-second glimpse, too—our bus screeching to a halt trying to avoid an oncoming bus around a hairpin curve—since I was asleep the first second. I am sure we've hit that bus or the guardrail or both, but we just back up, the driver and passengers making remarks in one of the world's 6,907 languages that I'll never know. (About one-fourth of the world's languages have fewer than a thousand remaining speakers, according to the Linguistic Society of America. Extinction of more than 3,000 is highly likely within the next century).

• • •

In the dreamy Dong village of Zhao Xing, I've finished a leisurely lunch and started a peaceful walk around town, expecting to talk to no one. But a surprising, "Hello, how are you, where are you from?" turns my head toward four schoolboys sitting on a street-side bench. They want to practice their English, and this might be their only chance to talk to a foreigner that year. One soon says, "Would you like to come to my village?" I never say no. "Do you want to walk an hour or take the bus?" he asks. I feel the four of them have a predilection for one over the other. I can be agreeable. I suggest we walk.

We walk endlessly, most of the time going up, and arrive in a village after one hour. But this is not it. After another 45 minutes, we enter Tang An ("tong-ON"). It is 5 p.m. Townspeople are congregating in the square. Eyes are upon us. Many faces have big smiles, it seems to me because some of their own kids have brought a foreigner to town. Perhaps they are pleased that someone from a faraway place feels their village is worth visiting. They don't seem to inquire of my friends where in the world I'm from.

It is getting dark, too late to venture back to Zhao Xing. A home rents a room to travelers. I get it for 25 yuan, a little over $3.00. I find out later the price also covers supper, including for the two students who are still with me, and my breakfast. We eat on the ground floor of the three-story home, and the TV is on. Townspeople come in by the twos and threes. The man on TV is speaking to an audience. According to one of my guides, the man is China's "king." Someday, perhaps, he'll learn the English word "president"—or one of the other titles the paramount leader has.

After dark, we while away time under the 13-level pagoda-like drum tower. Pounding the drum hanging down from the tower warns of a fire or an attack. The student instigator of my hike, Lu Zheyong, points out that the drum tower is bigger in Tang An than in the village we passed through. This seems to be a point of pride in the community. The larger town of Zhao Xing, where we started our hike, had three or four drum towers, each built by a different clan.

A teacher and his friend have been enjoying their Saturday afternoon. They invite Lu Zheyong, my other student guide Ou Gong Hua, and me to the teacher's house to party. We don't know whether to say yes or no, so we just go. Vegetables and bits of meat are prepared in one wok after another, finishing off with a handful of hot peppers. A bottle of something strong is opened. They make a toast. It is poetic, it has gusto, it is yelled out, and I might have it on a five-second video clip.

Sometime after the toast, the students show me back to the accommodation. Like most homes in the ethnic mountain villages, it is large and has three floors. One floor, often the ground floor, is the barn. In this home, though, the kitchen and living area are on the bottom floor. A hill on the side of the house gives the animals access to the second-floor barn. The toilet is an old wood bucket sitting on the barn floor next to the pigpen. My room is on the third floor.

In the middle of the night, I want to visit the old wood bucket one floor down. It is dark, and I've forgotten where the light switch is. I doubt whether I can find the bucket, assuming I don't tumble down the scarily steep stairs first.

To my surprise, however, I descend safely and make it quickly to the bucket—but not without bumping into the wooden pigpen and making the pig oink. All I need to do next is to spin 180 degrees and walk back to the stairs. They are nowhere to be found, though. The barn is pitch black. I feel my way around, but all I touch, sometimes noisily, are farm implements. I have to be quiet, wondering whether my making the pig OINK! OINK! will wake up the whole house. I think I might spend hours in the barn with the pig, for I don't want to yell for help. Nor could I. How do you yell out in Chinese, "I'm lost in the middle of the barn with the pig!" Luckily, on my third fumbling journey around the perimeter, I bump into the steps. My hard bed above couldn't feel better.

The next morning, I meander around town with Ou Gong Hua, my student-guide who is not from Tang An but is still hanging out with Lu Zheyong and me. Women talk to us, and he tells me what they are saying. One asks him where he is from; he names his distant village. Another asks him where I am from; America, he says. Another comments on how big I am. Two older women ask to try my glasses on. They both have the same comment: my glasses are "too" something for them. I'm not sure if they are too strong or too weak.

Later, Zheyong, Gong Hua, and I catch an infrequent bus back to Zhao Xing. Their Chinese teacher is hanging out of his second-floor window, and we are invited in for conversation. My two student guides and I then walk a mile to their school. Even though it is Sunday, we find some girls of high-school age in Gong Hua's 72-student classroom. We have a rigorous English lesson, during which I emphasize pronunciation. They also want me to provide the answers for a multiple-choice English assignment (which I do; oops!). The homework is for their first class of the week, which starts a few hours later—at 7 p.m. Sunday.

Right after we do their homework, we are outside shooting baskets. Two girls approach the court from the student dormitory with what seems to be large and luscious vanilla ice cream cones. How I'd love to have one right about now. But luscious cones they are not. The girls have peeled a vegetable, and that's what they are munching. Soon I am munching too. The vegetable tastes like a mild turnip. They give me several for my backpack. (I will be finishing them off in Kunming, watching US election results.)

The next day at 7 a.m., Ou Gong Hua and I exchange email addresses through my bus window. He and Lu Zheyong have come to wish me a safe journey. Will we ever exchange messages, let alone see each other again? Who knows. I then jot about the bus journey that began at 7:03 a.m.: "Slight rain, beautiful mountains, terraced farms, villages, school kids walking on new-paved road with umbrellas."

Tomorrow, I'll travel by bus to the ancient city of Dali on the road to Tibet. I've been assembling excessive amounts of foods and snacks. My backpack will be loaded with dried, darkened slices of lemon, tangerines, sunflower and pumpkin seeds, tiny green balls looking like miniature broccoli to make tea that's good for the throat and stomach, compacted balls of flowers I picked from tea bins, cake pieces from a hotel deli, and breads from the Muslim sector of Kunming.

And, from the schoolgirls on Sunday, delicious, irresistible vanilla ice cream cones that turn into turnips.

Get Good at Gong Fu—and Life
NOVEMBER 14, 2006

Dali, a city perhaps 2,000 years old on the far side of China, is one of my last stops. It's been attracting a new breed of visitor recently. A Chinese woman relaxing on a sunny café balcony will spend the warm winter here. Right now, she's reading a book. She's only 30 years old but has already made her money in the stock market. "How many years did you invest in the stock market?" I'm eager to know.

"Five," she answers.

As I hike on top of the south wall that encloses Old Dali, a sign near a pagoda issues a strong invitation partly in English: "Training supplied to improve your Gong Fu quickly. Gong Fu includes Jingang boxing, Baxian boxing, animal boxing (contains: peacock, centipede, spider, frog, snake), Taiha boxing, monkey boxing, drunk boxing, Bagua sword, Liuhe broadsword, spear, and stick." You're informed that later, you may be able to participate in a national competition. I think I'll go for the centipede boxing and fast, in case it's on the card for the 2008 Olympic Games in Beijing. How about you? The key to success will be in finding a centipede that's good on its feet.

To serve the influx of tourists—mostly Chinese—many young people have moved to Dali. At the Dragon Bar, which is more of a café, most of the nine workers have come from distant regions. Wei Lei, who speaks some English, says he lives 50 to 60 hours away by train. One night, I see him very sad and tearing when talking to his manager and coworkers. The next day, I pry out of him why: he misses his family and girlfriend—and probably can't go home to visit them.

I explain to Wei Lei the words "nutrition" and "nutritionist" and discuss recent recommendations that Americans eat five to nine servings of fruits and vegetables a day. (Chinese seem to eat many servings of both.) "Do you think Americans eat enough fruits and vegetables every day?" I inquire.

"I think Americans eat enough meat every day," he comments.

Wei Lei is a graduate from a top university in Beijing. Universities can financially help only a few of the needy who pass the entrance exam, though. "Can university students discuss the Beijing Tiananmen Square massacre when many were killed protesting for democracy in 1989?" I ask.

"Yes, we can talk about it, and professors can say things."

"But don't they have to be careful?"

"No, not like before. But the papers they write won't be published."

And with that, we move on.

"You single traveler, you don't have fear traveling here?" Wei Lei inquires. "Because in most countries some people are bad."

"No, I don't have fear," I tell him.

He dreams of backpacking in foreign countries, like he sees foreigners doing in China. Wei Lei tells me in another conversation that "Chinese hate Bush and hate Japan for what it did in 1939." Coworker Dong Hang Fei provides live entertainment, although the owner never requested it and probably doesn't even know, since she's usually absent. When he's not busy inside or standing in front of the café urging passersby to drop in, he's in the narrow street performing martial arts kicks above his head, dribbling a basketball, strumming a guitar, singing along with the music the Dragon pumps out, or dancing by himself. One night, he rollerblades out of the café and down the street. He is back within a couple minutes with one roller half falling off. He sits down, takes them off, marches to a rubbish can, and heaves them in with a sense of accomplishment, not disappointment. Perhaps a tourist has discarded them.

With interpreter Wei Lei's help, I tell multitalented, energetic Dong Hang Fei how positive it is that he persistently learns and displays new skills. And that he thus brightens the lives of many. He seems both pleased and shy to hear this. He does, however, have a response: "Life is beautiful."

Tiger Leaping Gorge
NOVEMBER 18, 2006

Leaving Dali, bus rides carry me to Lijiang and beyond. I step down near a guest house at the entrance to Tiger Leaping Gorge. The next morning, a French gentleman asks whether I am prepared for my hike onward and upward, with boots and a walking stick. "No, and no," I answer with concern. With that clue in mind, I find a woman selling bamboo walking sticks early in my trek. She helps pick one out that costs 5 yuan—60 cents.

Many people are to admire my stick, whose flattened "Y" handle resembles an animal head, perhaps a goat's. The handle was the bamboo's root. First to comment is a man who has probably lived his life here. I ride his horse 20 minutes up the steep "18 Bends" for a small fee. A Chinese hiker calls the stick a "piece of art." I won't be able to just toss it out when, and if, I complete the hike. I tell one and all that I will cut the stick in pieces to fit in my backpack for the plane ride home, glue it back together, and hang it on a wall at Lost Lake. (The stick is still in pieces in my closet at home; I have work to do.)

Far above the river that blasts through the gorge, the Half Way Guest House faces the snowcapped 17,703-foot Ha Ba Snow Mountains. It is a good place to sleep the first night. I've invested nine hours in that day's hike, but I stopped enough and marveled. Feng De Fang, a traditional medicine healer, owns the house. He began taking in hikers in 1992, when the first foreigners pleaded for a meal and a place to sleep. His family settled in these mountains seven generations before, after leaving Sichuan Province to escape invaders. The first generation lived in a cave.

Walking the trail the next day, I am jolted out of my traveler's trance by sudden noises. I first think I must have startled goats, who perceive hikers as nemeses. Looking ahead, however, I spot cantaloupe-sized rocks bounding across my trail and down the gorge at an excessive speed. They might've broken loose at the top and are halfway finished with a descent of 12,434 feet to the river, picking up speed the whole way. My attention diverted, the main trail goes one way as I drift another. My personal path soon peters into an imaginary track the width of a 10D shoe. Overcoming my fear, I venture back across the route of tumbling stones to locate the real trail.

The river far below has to me been nameless. On the second day, I happen to read that it is the Jinsha, a primary tributary of the upper Yangtze. Like most hikers, I never do descend to the Jinsha at the bottom of the gorge.

Off-the-beaten-track travelers hike Tiger Leaping Gorge because, as touted by a tour office, it's "one of the deepest and most spectacular river canyons in the world"—and a Top 10 Trek of Asia. A Chinese corporate lawyer and her husband who distributes Wilsonart counter-tops slow to chat with me, as does a young man who left his job exporting clothing to the US so he could travel his country for four months.

Over half the people in China, at the time of this visit, reside in rural and even remote areas, like the older man in a Mao cap and animal skin vest on the trail. He hands me an apple but won't accept a Snickers bar in return, all communications conducted by hand signal and facial expressions. He thinks my camera video of him hiking this age-old trail is a riot, as do I. He is likely a member of the Naxi indig-enous culture. If we spoke a common language, I'd have asked him to lead me to the spot where a tiger, escaping from a hunter, leapt across the river at the gorge's narrowest point—82 feet. And I'd inquire about the legend of the leaping tiger.

Oh, would I have loved to speak the Naxi man's language. I have no idea what I might've learned, but I'd be telling you right now. Perhaps I was subconsciously recalling the letter sent to me by a Peace Corps Volunteer school teacher working in a village far from Kathmandu.[19] He'd written about "interesting, peculiar discoveries of the day [like]

---

[19] See "Why Do You Love the Other Worlds So?"

everyone's name has a meaning, the relative order of casts, what happens when people die [and] how to set a broken arm . . ."

Descending on the Tiger Leaping Gorge trail and disappearing from the Naxi man's life, I check in at the Tibetan Guest House late on the second afternoon for a meal and card-playing with an Australian family and three young engineering graduates from England. The next morning, the Sydney family and I bundle into the guest house's minivan for a ride to Quiaotou, a town toward Lijiang. On a curve, we sideswipe an oncoming truck carrying 40 concrete power poles. Our windshield goes to pieces, and we end up in the ditch, but not one of us is injured.

After we get a lift to Quiaotou, the van to Lijiang runs out of gas five minutes short of a gas station. A small truck arrives the same day, carrying gas in an open-topped container resembling a kettle. In a hop, skip, and transoceanic jump, I then hit Lijiang, Shenzen, Hong Kong, and Hibbing, Minnesota, ending 38 days in Asia.

A Top 10 Trek in Asia—Tiger Leaping Gorge in Western China, with the Ha Ba Snow Mountains across the gorge.

Making a Naxi friend without the benefit of words while hiking in Tiger Leaping Gorge. He gave Tom an apple, but did not accept a Snickers bar in return.

Return to China
THE YEAR 2010

In the years following my 2006 visit to the Dong ethnic village of Tang On, I'd heard from Ou Gong Hua, the student who had been one of my guides. He'd informed me that the village of Tang On had burned down—in spite of its 13-level Drum Tower useful to warn residents of a fire or an attack. He'd lost touch with Lu Zheyong and didn't know how he was. Come 2010, I was toying with another trip to Asia. So I wrote Ou Gong Hua.

OCTOBER 10

Hello Ou Gong Hua, how are you? Are you at home or at the university in Zhanjiang? It is possible I can come to China. If you are going to Zhanjiang, when will you be there?

OCTOBER 16

Dear Tom, I very happy to hear you will come to again, welcome to China! Now I at the university in Zhanjiang, It my university in the city, I in October and November during the day in the Zhanjiang. Zhanjiang (湛江) from Nanning (南宁) can on the train. Nanning is a beautiful city, beautiful scenery, the sunlight is temperate, and the weather is very temperate. Zhanjiang is a harbor city, it in the mainland China most south tip. I in university's specialty is the Veterinary Medicine—veterinarian.

Note to my Washington, DC, friend
OCTOBER 23

Hi Dan, I'm tapping away in a 50-computer internet café at 30 cents an hour. Across the street is a 20,000-student university and its magnificent, spacious campus in Zhanjiang, China's far southeast. I've visited a friend from 2006 who's now a veterinary student. We bicycled around a campus lake in a dense subtropical park. I visited his dorm of a thousand students and met his five roommates, each of course with his own personality. They study, banter, wash clothes, play basketball and volleyball, and are proud of the NBA's Yao Ming. I hope to get into Laos from Southern China next week.

OCTOBER 27

Dear Tom, Where are you now? Do you in Dali or Laos? Dali is certainly very beautiful! Hoped you are joyful in that! I am very good in the school, my classmates very much think of you, they asked me where are you in? Your friend, Ou Hua

OCTOBER 28

Dear Gong Hua, I had a great time visiting you and your university. It was educational. I'm now in Jinghong in the Xishuangbanna region of China. It is south of Kunming in Yunnan Province. Yesterday I traveled by bus from Jinghong to a small town, Xiding, for a Thursday market. I'm not sure what language they speak in Xiding. On market day, perhaps three or four languages are spoken. I'll leave China for Laos soon.

Market Day in Xiding
OCTOBER 28, 2010

If you like to shoot pool and play cards and gamble and smoke, there's a perfect place for you in Xiding. Even if you're just a 10-year-old boy like us—girls choose other venues for their activities. It's Thursday, and the town in the subtropical monsoon mountains is full of visitors buying, selling, and eating in the streets. Over 100 motorcycles have arrived.

As 10-year-olds, we don't drink alcohol in this place. We leave that up to the old men sitting around the table outside, them and their homemade brew and smoking. We've got two pool tables and we keep them busy all day. We don't pay any attention to the hole in one pool table pocket that drops balls on the floor. We or one of the older players, say age 15, just pick the ball up, getting it out from among the dusty pumpkins, empty beer bottles, and an almost empty bowl of noodles that's been there under the table for what looks like days, chopsticks neatly placed on top.

A stranger walks into our pool hall real slow. He says nothing except "good morning" when one of our 12-year-old friends tests his knowledge of English with "good morning." We know our friend hopes the stranger doesn't say anything else, because our friend only knows two or three words in that very foreign language. The stranger seems to understand and says not a word more.

The stranger studies our game like he's writing a book. Little do we know that even after watching everything that's going on for quite some time, he doesn't have a clue how the game works. It's so simple, we think. We play pool. We use a deck of cards at the same time, and each of the four players has a hand. When the winning twosome is determined, the losers throw money on the pool table. Before the winners can pick it up, though, the owner appears and exacts his share. The game then starts anew. How is it that the stranger doesn't have a clue what game we're playing?

Meanwhile, the stranger is astute enough to see that we boys are not playing with a full deck, since we are three pool balls short of normal. He also observes that very little conversation takes place. A great shot or a rotten shot usually draws no comment. It's almost strangely quiet. Is it, he wonders, because with so many in town today from neighboring villages, each player has his own language? He realizes that none of the words seem to be in Chinese. Some might be Dai or Akha. Xiding is in China, but few if anyone here is ethnic Chinese. (The country's national language is Mandarin Chinese, based on the dialect of the Han ethnic group.)

Without a word, the stranger slips slowly out of the pool hall. He buys bananas. He passes on the hundreds of other items for sale, including false teeth, one or two of which can be installed in a market-goer's mouth as he or she sits on a stool between sandals and grains.

Now the out-of-towner makes his way down the hill, hoping the only bus that will leave town before tomorrow hasn't departed yet. He learns, however, that the bus is gone. He hangs around wondering if there's another way to go back down the mountains to Jinghong, a most appealing city with a tropical monsoon climate. As he fiddles away his time, he gazes at the mountains yonder that might be in Burma. An hour later, a minivan driver spots the foreigner's predicament, stops, and squeezes him into the vehicle. The driver knows at least two words in English: "No money." The traveler arrives fare-free in Jinghong before the tropical sundown.

LAOS

Into Laos from China
NOVEMBER 5, 2010

After crossing over a remote border from China, I jump on a 100 cc Honda motorbike and weave two hours through the mountains to Muang Sing, an old French Indochina outpost. They say it's in the heart of the Golden Triangle. A girl of 13 or 14 waves me and my rented Honda down on the way back. As soon as she jumps on behind me, other kids want to join us. Since I don't know how to say "no way" in Lao or their ethnic language, I just wave them away and speed by. Perhaps they are all walking miles home from school. The girl taps my shoulder later on, signaling she'll get off at a side road that runs to her village. As we chat in sign language for a minute, I snap a most beautiful photograph.

This girl has hitched a motorbike ride in the heart of the Golden Triangle of Northern Laos, and will now walk down a side road to her village. Other children near the old French Indochina outpost of Muang Sing, seeing that the girl was picked up, waved for the motorbikers to stop for them, too.

I'm now in my favorite Laotian town. Luang Prabang has changed a lot since I visited in 2004. Little do I know that *The New York Times* named it

the best place in the world to visit in 2006 and 2008, this according to a Pennsylvania woman who lives here. Now hundreds of small merchants sell village handicrafts—Hmong among several others. Restaurants, hotels, upscale guest houses, and gift shops abound. Coffee, mango shakes, chocolate chip cookies, and croissants from French Indochina recipes are consumed at cafés overlooking the Mekong River or the other river cutting through town whose name I may learn. At night, dozens of vendors pack a long alley barbequing river fish, chicken, and pork chops, or urging visitors to fill a plate from an array of vegetarian foods for $1.25. I need Lao money, of course, but decide I'll just get 2,400,000 to start. It takes awhile to burn through a million, but it's fun. (The million equals $125).

Graceful Buddhist temples dot the town, one from 1560. Novice monks study at each one. I return to a temple at 4 p.m., since a student tells me the moon is full and they'll be drumming. I listen as a robed student drums away on a suspended drum. The option I pass on is to come back at 4 a.m. the next morning.

After hearing that a hotel worker's village is just 60 kilometers away, I assume that he can return home often. Until I learn that's not practical, since he must walk the last 13 km—"it's just a path." A restaurant worker has tomorrow afternoon off. He'll pick me up on his motorbike, and we'll ride to a most beautiful, cascading waterfall "and then go to my village, if you want." His is a Khmu village. We won't have to walk 13 km. We'll just ride into town, like no one in history ever did until a few years ago.

I'll now look for ways to burn another million like it's going out of style.

The Bridge over the River Khan
NOVEMBER 10, 2010

The disillusionment over the great advances in the traveler's favorite Asian town is beginning to subside. How can it not, for he can now sit at an outdoor table looking down on the river that flows into the Mekong just around the bend, drink superb coffee from Arthouse Café, and read the *Straits Times* carried in from Singapore the night before by the café's Canadian owner.

Ensconced at Arthouse with steaming coffee, he watches as a foot bridge over the wide river below is bound together piece by piece. What's on the other side? He can only see farm patches running up the river bank and two rooflines showing through the trees, perhaps belonging to a Buddhist temple. Day by day, the bamboo and wood bridge is fastened together by kneeling and crouching figures. Should a semi-inquisitive traveler guess what barely beckons on the other side, or go?

He descends the riverbank. A man still working on the narrow bridge approaches, collects the 50-cent toll, and hands him a ticket that says, "For Two Way." He just has to make sure to come back before the rainy season, when the builders deconstruct the bridge so it doesn't get washed into the Mekong and perhaps beached in Thailand, Cambodia, or Vietnam, or spat out into the South China Sea.

Bamboo footbridge over the River Khan as it is reconstructed after the rainy season has ended. The Khan joins the Mekong River just downstream, and together they move toward the distant South China Sea.

Now on the bridge, saffron-robed student monks pass him up. He trails behind. A friend of theirs wading in the shallow water on the other shore throws a net and captures minnow-like fish. A half-dozen long canoes rest along the bank. One floats downriver, carrying a throw-net fisherman who must be standing, of course, to do his job.

The monk students, called novices, do not take the only discernible path up the riverbank. The traveler asks himself whether he should take the path or follow in the novices' footsteps. This is a fork in the road inside the traveler's head, one of many he confronts every day. The novices, followed by the traveler, walk through a garden lush with cabbage and broccoli. A woman and man carrying sprinkler cans water the hillside crops. The entourage edges around the farm couple's rough house built on stilts and walks past a black-masked boy conquering the world with martial arts moves. Farther up is the temple.

Monk novices in the window of their room at a Buddhist temple on the far side of the River Khan in Luang Prabang, Laos.

Luang Prabang students stop briefly to greet a visitor, and then motorbike to school.

The monk novices now engage the traveler. As usual, one speaks more English than the others. "What about taking photos?" the traveler asks. He's told that it's OK. This *wat* (or temple) does not sit alone but is part of a busy little town invisible to a reader of the *Straits Times* on the other side of the river. After photos at the wat and a stroll around the once-invisible town, the traveler uses his two-way ticket to return to Luang Prabang.

The days go by and could last forever but for a Thanksgiving engagement at his cousin Marvin's home near the shores of Lake Superior in Minnesota. As it always does, the last day arrives. By chance, the traveler spots a Kodak shop. A hundred inexpensive prints in hand, he makes the rounds again to share them, under threat of a plane-to-Hanoi departure. Across the toll bridge again, through the farmer's garden, by his house on stilts—slowly because a chat with him is in order—and on to the temple and the novices. The traveler, always wondering, doesn't know whether the monk students may own worldly possessions like color photos of themselves. Apparently, they may. They are quite happy upon seeing them. Perhaps they'll adorn the sparse shack that will be their home for years, far away from their remote villages. These novices' families and village friends may also enjoy a glimpse of these photos later this year, when the future monks travel home for a visit.

Now back again across the footbridge to Joma Café, giving dozens of photos to three friends who invited him to a karaoke bar and traditional

At the Kuang Si Waterfalls near Luang Prabang, one aqua pool cascades to the next. One is tempted to float in each of them. And may.

barbeque dinners on the Mekong riverbank. Not only that, but they also explored one of the traveler's favorite swimming spots in the world, Kuang Si Waterfalls, which cascade endlessly from one aqua pool to the next. The friends at Joma Café agree to take the previous day's photos of a girl who lives across the street and two other wonderfully stylish teenage girls to them, saving the traveler some time.

The traveler next moves on to Saffron Café. He hands out prints to a worker who invited him to the king's palace, which lost its function in 1975 when Pathet Lao revolutionaries were victorious and sent the royal family to live in a cave. (Khun Lo, the legendary founder of Luang Prabang, died in 780 A.D.) There are still photos to give, and given they are to those who work at the traveler's guest house or nearby.

Now, the traveler is ready to leave the Mekong and the bridge over the River Khan and the temple-filled town of Luang Prabang. He may come back in a couple years, suffer another bout of disillusionment, and settle in for endless days, months, or several Lao new years.

VIETNAM, or VIET NAM, or VIET-NAM

(as variously spelled in the early stages of the war)

The War
NOVEMBER 11, 2010

Sabadee, Linda,

I'm about to fly Lao Airlines out of Luang Prabang and visit Vietnam for a week, before heading back to China for the flight home. I'm figuring out a schedule that includes historic sites from the Vietnam War, though I believe most people here call it the "American War" or the "Second Indochina War." The sites might include the DMZ, Khe Sahn battlefield, the old city of Hue, and Da Nang, once home to a huge US airbase. I traveled in the Saigon environs during the war in 1971.[20] This time I'll focus on the northern half of the country now known as the Socialist Republic of Vietnam.

Hanoi, Vietnam
NOVEMBER 12, 2010

Hi Eddie,

I arrived in Hanoi minutes ago. On the way in from the airport, I tasted the crazy traffic—a vehicle nudged a motorbike to the side, which

[20] Flip back to "Around the World in 400 Days" for that story.

nudged another bike. The bikes stopped for a second just to hold each other up, then moved on. In the first couple days in China, I was nudged three times by a bicycle or motorbike, once when I was on a motorbike as a passenger, my backpack up on the gas tank. All them nudges left no marks.

Hoi An
NOVEMBER 15, 2010

Rainy Hoi An, on Thu Bon River near the South China Sea in central Vietnam, was settled about two thousand years ago and was a top Asian trading port two to four centuries ago. In Hoi An's heyday of international trade, Vietnamese ceramics, silk, and hardwood made their way to other Asian countries, Egypt, and Europe. Many languages are now heard on the streets, because Hoi An has become an international travel destination.

The delivery man's work never stops in rainy Hoi An on the South China Sea.

The occupant of a private home I stepped into is the eighth generation of her family to reside there. Two or three times a year around this time, she says, everything on the ground floor must be lifted to the second floor through a trap door, because flood waters are often five feet deep on the first floor. (Last night, I noticed the rising river was six inches below street level.)

One must visit old community halls that were

also places of worship used by Chinese residents and traders. The halls are Vietnam's version of the old immigrant Finnish Kaleva Halls in Minnesota, California, and other states (although Kaleva Halls lack altars for worship). I explore every part of the multiroomed hall established by people from Canton. I am the only visitor. The older gentleman who mans the hall says that today, 25% of this town's residents are of Chinese ethnicity.

P.S. I take another curious look at the Thu Bon River. It's gone over its banks and flooded nearby streets. The residents are unperturbed—boating, motorbiking, and wading. After shelling out $2 to replace my 50-cent raincoat and another $2 for thongs, I stick my shoes and socks in my backpack and walk many a flooded street. Finding the back door of the Cargo Club open, I sit down for breakfast—warm croissants, several rolls, juice, strong coffee, and a fruit plate, all for $2.75. You just can't leave by the other door, not because

Visiting the lone attendant in Hoi An's multi-roomed community hall built by, and for, immigrants and traders from the Canton region of China.

cargo is coming in, *a la* 1760, but because that street runs along, and now under, the risen river. Besides, walking out that door and down the steps to the submerged pavement, you might not know where the other side of the street ends and the river begins, and then it'll be, Goodbye Vietnam, Good Morning South China Sea.

The Propagandist and His Elite Brother
NOVEMBER 20, 2010

If you cut Vietnam in the middle and hang out there for a week, you can't go wrong. After getting your feet wet in the flood-prone city of Hoi An, visit a city called Da Nang and the Cham Museum, highlighting a civilization that peaked before the 12th century. In another museum, learn how the Mongols invaded Vietnam in 1288 with an armada of epic proportions.

Epic, too, was the arrival beginning 675 years later of 2,707,918 American troops—9.7% of their generation—most setting foot at the Da Nang base (Cam Ranh Bay, Plieku, and Tan Son Nhut were among other air bases used for combat purposes by the US). A total of 58,220 Americans died, and another 304,000 were wounded. It is likely that the death toll among Vietnamese civilians and soldiers in the South and North was at least 1.3 million, and perhaps much higher. Today, note the march of globalization in Da Nang, with a Hyatt development on China Beach and a nearby Chevy dealer.

Continue north to Hue, still below the middle. My memory tells me only that Hue was "old" and was a "battleground" in the "Vietnam War." "Old," I've just learned, in that the emperor built a foreboding Forbidden City enclosed by moats and thick walls in the early 1800s. The royal family and hundreds of soldiers, mandarins, and hangers-on lived there until the last emperor abdicated in 1945. "Battleground," I now remember, in that the North Vietnamese and Viet Cong overran Hue during the 1968 Tet Offensive and planted their flag at the grand entrance to the old imperial palace grounds. Winning it was deadly for them; winning it back was just as deadly for the other side, with door-to-door and room-to-room combat. As for the "Vietnam War," it is usually called the "American War" here or, in one museum, the "Anti-American War."

You may now walk freely through the emperor's old grounds. I'd suggest you visit the Ho Chi Minh Museum on the opposite side of the Perfume River. A block away is the Quoc Hoc High School where Ho Chi Minh was a student until he was expelled for taking part in antigovernment demonstrations. His work against colonialism started earlier, in 1899, when at age 9 he became a messenger for an anticolonial organization. He learned six languages and was a major historical force for decades. He died in Hanoi in 1969. After the war ended, Saigon was renamed Ho Chi Minh City.

I roll the dice and enter Ho's school grounds, which is like a small college campus. I just want to enroll in a couple of history classes but am stopped after taking only a peek. If I read the gatekeeper right, he is saying no to my idea because Americans don't learn from history anyway. I settle for hopping on the Reunification Express train north for a night in Dong Ha.

• • •

The alarm clock gets a rise out of me at 6 a.m. I walk across Vietnam's north-south highway that splits Dong Ha in half. I sit down half asleep on a low plastic stool at a low plastic table. I see the hot, sweet coffee dripping into a glass on the counter, not yet served. A little girl looks at me like I'm a stranger. A little boy looks at me like the girl did. The café is full. Most are young, but two old men walk in and sit near me. I am out of place. With no coffee in my bloodstream yet, I realize groggily that I'm sitting a few miles south of the old De-Militarized Zone that separated North and South Vietnam. I'm about to visit places seared into the memory of many, not only the old men of Dong Ha next to me, but people the world over. A bus of Vietnamese and Europeans stops in front. An American is thus added to the mix. I take a seat next to the guide. (Who knows what family secrets a guide might whisper into your ear?)

We look toward a peak called Rock Pile. US soldiers helicoptered to the top to direct artillery strikes because no roads climbed the steep sides, nor do any today. We continue heading parallel to the old DMZ in the direction of Laos. What appears to be a sandy path along a river is a remnant of the Ho Chi Minh Trail, an elaborate system for the infiltration of troops and supplies from North Vietnam to South Vietnam.

We now turn northerly to a place the world heard about every day in early 1968: Khe Sanh. It was a US military base. US intelligence concluded the North Vietnamese were massing for an attack. President Lyndon Johnson increased the troop and materiel level astronomically because he "didn't want a damn Dien Bien Phu," the fateful battle the French had lost in Indochina to 40,000 Vietnamese troops in 1954.

The 1968 battle at Khe Sanh, in which 6,000 US Marines held off 20,000 North Vietnamese troops for 77 days, was one of the costliest, with 155 Americans killed and another 425 wounded. With US attention focused on Khe Sanh, the North Vietnamese and Viet Cong had more freedom, just as they planned, to launch the Tet Offensive all across South Vietnam. The North Vietnamese then disappeared from the hills around Khe Sahn. Three months later, the US blew up its defensive fortifications and abandoned Khe Sanh, just as it repeatedly abandoned hilltop after hilltop after valiant and deadly attempts at micro-occupation.

Fifty years later, US presidential historian Michael Beschloss wrote about the dirty secret that US commanders, fearful of losing the battle at Khe Sanh, were planning to arm US forces in Vietnam with nuclear weapons. President Lyndon Johnson disrupted the plan and ordered the operational documents locked up, perhaps never to see the light of day. But they eventually emerged—in 2018.

Today, you can stare at the old Khe Sanh runway through a padlocked, rusting chain-link fence. A Boeing Chinook helicopter looks almost operational. A few American bunkers have been repaired for effect. Coffee trees have been planted. It rains off and on at Khe Sanh today. Central Vietnam hasn't seen the sun in days.

Heading back to Dong Ha for a turn north across the DMZ, we're eager to explore the Vinh Moc tunnels in the mountain above the ocean. Villagers in the north built miles of tunnels at three different depths to hide and even live in for days on end during US bombing. We hunch down and walk through the maze. We exit one tunnel, see the sea below us, and walk in another. A sign says a side tunnel was a maternity ward. One bomb penetrated 30 feet and breached a tunnel. It was not filled in. Instead, it functioned as tunnel ventilation.

Sitting next to the guide on the bus, I ask whether American Vietnam veterans join her tours. "Yes. With a son, daughter, spouse, or in a group. Sometimes, the son or daughter of a vet who doesn't want to come back will visit and take a video home for their dad," the guide tells me.

"Do your parents or grandparents talk about the war?" I ask, since she seems too young to have firsthand memories. She tells me of her oldest brother who was a propagandist for the South Vietnamese government. Another brother had different ideas, though. At age 14 or 15, he began helping the Viet Cong guerillas of South Vietnam. He later moved to North Vietnam, joined its army, and rose up to the elite ranks.

"What was this brother's motivation?" I asked.

"He said, 'Vietnam is for the Vietnamese, not the Americans.' He said the Vietnamese threw out the Chinese after centuries, defeated the French, beat the Japanese, defeated the French again at Dien Bien Phu, and now they would expel the Americans. He argued that the South Vietnamese government was a puppet of the United States."

"Well," I inquire, "what propaganda did your other brother propagandize?"

"He argued that the South Vietnamese government did good things for the people. And it was not communist." My guide continued: "After the North Vietnamese won the war in 1975, my anticommunist brother in the South was sent to a reeducation camp. My brother in the victorious North, however, put in a word for the other one, who was released after just a year."

"Do the brothers get along now?" I inquire.

"The whole family gets together at important functions," she answers. "In Vietnam, we all meet at the time of death of a parent. We worship our parents. These brothers scream at each other when historical or political issues come up. The one in the north is retired from the army and lives in Hanoi. The one in the south works for a gas company in Saigon and can't risk expressing anticommunist views."

"What about the brothers' children?" I now want to know.

My guide says they all get along great and have fun together.

"What about the brothers' grandchildren?"

"They are focused on jobs and the economy and computers. They don't know what happened between the grandfathers. And I don't think they would understand!"

Since I can't get enrolled in Ho Chi Minh's old school in Hue, I'll have to settle for the above synopsis of Vietnamese history, as influenced by outside forces, from 1288 to 2010. I hope to read someone else's synopsis, covering 2010 to 2030. If you visit or work in Vietnam in the coming decades, let me know. I hope to post your contribution on this book's website, TomsGlobe.com.

Forgetting My Passport
NOVEMBER 21, 2010

Hi Leo,

Today I crossed into China from Hanoi by van. It took a day longer than I'd planned. Approaching the Chinese border yesterday, I realized I'd left my passport at a Hanoi hotel. That van arrived at the border minus me, who was unexpectedly returning to Hanoi by bus. Today, I managed to stay aboard all the way to the border. I'm now heading to an airport here in Southern China to fly north over most of China (likely covered in smog up to 20,000 or 25,000 feet). I'll change planes in Beijing, head north of Siberia and Alaska (jetting closer to the North Pole than to Anchorage), and keep curving, so when we touch down, hopefully we're on one of those O'Hare runways.

Circumnavigating the Right Way

Hey Leo,

My message told you the jet will fly north of Siberia and Alaska and keep curving to Chicago. I just realized that a plane flying that route will go in a *straight line*. All the way. Check it out on a globe. Then I'll be within miles of your spot on that sphere after 45 days in Japan, China, Laos, and Vietnam.

Heavenly Blessing Your Health, Joyful Daily

NOVEMBER 26, 2010

Dear Tom,

I have two weeks already not accessed the net. I thought your place had snowed now, you and your friend makes a small house in the lake for you to fish. I hope you live joyfully. I am go to play basketball in the afternoon, jogged exercises the body. Last night the Asian Games man basketball plays in the finals China and South Korea. My many schoolmates also looking it. Not have to be NBA to be attractive. It is most worth the competition. This competition has the cohesive force very much, we refuel before the television for the Chinese team. We deeply love our mother-land! The day before yesterday was Thanksgiving Day. Now I pray for heavenly blessing your health, joyful daily.

Your, Ou Gong Hua

Dear Gong Hua,

Yes, it is snowing and cold. The ice on the lakes is still thin. No one is walking on it yet. In three weeks, the fishermen will tow their fishing houses onto the lakes. On Thanksgiving, I drove an hour through forests to my cousin Marvin and Irene's house in Two Harbors, Minnesota—on Lake Superior. Lebron James and the Miami Heat have won four or five straight games, as you probably know. Christmas is coming December 25.

Your friend, Tom

• • •

In later years, I'd still hear from Ou Gong Hua. By 2019, after working in "remote mountainous areas to help the poor," he became the official veterinary surgeon at an animal health institute. "I am now the father of two daughters. I bought a house but haven't finished decorating it yet. Young people in China are mostly fighting for their houses, you should know," he recently wrote.

Thus continues a friendship that began in 2006, when I heard young voices call to me as I explored the ethnic town of Zhao Xing, voices that I heard for hours as we climbed to the village of Tang An, voices I heard the next day too—but voices that were nowhere to be heard in the dead of night when I was lost in the middle of a pitch-black barn with the pig.[21]

What experiences I would have missed in China in 2006 and 2010 and through written communications had the students not called out to me on a Zhao Xing street—and had I not turned and listened.

---

[21] Flip back to "The Pitch-Black Barn and Turnip Ice Creams" if you'd like a refresher.

NEW YORK CITY
CITY
and
LONDON

NEW YORK CITY

Tales of Strange in a Large City
JANUARY 17, 2016

strangers in the night

It seems remarkable to me that a man calling himself Jasper keeps showing up in my life unexpectedly—like now, in New York City. [22]

The F, the M, and the B, D, and L Trains all come plunging through the cavernous subway station at 14th Street and Sixth Avenue. It's Saturday midnight, and Mark is searching for the F train downtown.

Mark has a lot on his mind. He lives here in New York City but also resides in Boston, where he works, and in Philadelphia, where he goes to college. Mark helps run the United Nations by organizing debates and travel, after a fashion. Specifically, he leads American student groups who participate in UN mock debates. They travel to Beijing, Budapest, and India. A young American debater may take the role of China's UN representative and argue the Chinese point of view. That student might win the debate and have a leg up on being accepted by a top American university.

Right now, though, at five minutes after midnight, Mark sees a man reading the *Wall Street Journal*; he must live right here in Manhattan. Mark asks the midnight reader if the F train downtown stops at this platform. "Yes, it does," Jasper says. They get on the next train and talk above the whirring of steel wheels on old tracks. Mark listens, pinpointing the newspaper reader as originally from Wisconsin.

---

[22] All names in this tell-all tale are changed except for Giants of the 20th Century and John Q. Public.

"Close, but can you zero in more than that?" the reader asks.

Mark seems to know. "Minnesota."

The Minnesotan gets off at East Broadway at 20 after midnight, newspaper in back pocket. He has a bed between the old Tenement District and Chinatown.

Jasper has never explored the trendy nightlife neighborhood of Williamsburg in Brooklyn, so one evening he's back on the F Train. At the corner of York and Sixth, while stuffing his coffee cup cover into the recyclables drum, he's interrupted by two college-age women. They need directions.

"I'm just visiting," Jasper demurs, before asking where they're from.

"We're from Westchester County. One hour north. In the woods. And where are you from?"

"I'm from two days west," Jasper answers, "on a frozen lake. It's swimmable in the summertime."

After leaving a Manhattan museum another evening, Jasper ducks into a Hilton Hotel, looking for *The New York Times*. On the café lunch counter, he only sees *USA Today* and the *Wall Street Journal*. He asks the cashier where the *Times* is sold. Speaking with a heavy Italian accent, the cashier doesn't say where but offers Jasper the counter papers for free. "Take both. You decide! Which is the one that is the better writer!" Jasper takes both. He likes every written word.

Days later, Jasper (Jas to some friends) meets up with neighborhood friend Mikko Aarilla from Palo, in the ethnic heart of their home state. It is the first time that Mikko prowls a city of this size. At 15 to midnight, Mikko pauses, inhaling history outside The Bitter End at 147 Bleecker Street, a club open since 1961. In halcyon days, Bob Dylan, Joni Mitchell, James Taylor, Allen Ginsberg, Stevie Wonder, Kris Kristofferson, Woody Allen, and other young artists named Peter, Paul, and Mary all performed there.

At five to midnight, Mikko is munching inside an old-line Greenwich Village Italian pizza joint. On a wall clock, he sees that the current time in Italy is 5:55 a.m. Mikko makes an instantaneous decision, perhaps unprecedented for Greenwich Village, halcyon days or not (unlike a young Woody Allen gripped by stage fright who— it's said—tried to flee The Bitter End through a window just before a comedy performance). Without so much as announcing his intention, Mikko belts out the famed "*Funiculì, Funiculà*" in Italian, in the way he's performed songs in different languages in his home state.

This midnight Greenwich Village performance is for a surprised audience of five—including the two Egyptian-American pizzeria workers. The pair, with the broadest smiles of their 10-hour shifts, record Mikko's performance on their smartphones, making him start over so they can catch it in full. The three customers appreciate the robust rendition too. Mikko then disappears into the Saturday night's madding crowds. His performance the next day is at the iconic out-door fountain at Lincoln Center. The passersby clap their hands, and not just to stay warm in the winter cold.

unusual (retrospectively)

Jasper's addiction to visiting the large city like no other started at an earlier age. As everyone in his family grew older, his mother reminded him that, at age 16, he'd driven a '58 Chevy like a savvy New Yorker through the streets of Manhattan during a family car trip. In visits a couple of decades later, he'd mention Woodstock to New Yorkers; many responded they'd heard about the event that August of 1969 "but could not go." During that summer, Jas had been working at 52 Wall Street. Like millions of New Yorkers, he had not been able to go either. It was also the summer when the raiding police were fought off by the Stonewall Inn bar patrons.

While Jasper was enjoying a beer on a Greenwich Village bar stool on a July evening that summer of '69, a customer came up and ordered drinks for his table's threesome. An hour earlier, Jasper and a table-mate at a nearby basement folk music club had noticed the threesome taking in a performance by 22-year-old Loudon Wainwright III (a future father of three musicians). "Hey Bob," Jas now said to the man ordering at the bar, "I'm from Biwabik." Jasper's was not a shot in the dark. Only one "Bob" out of about 91,000 in New York was familiar with Biwabik, Minnesota, it's safe to say. This was the one New York Bob who knew Biwabik, because he had left his nearby mining town of Hibbing 10 years earlier for bigger cities—and then world fame as Bob Dylan.

Even today on a languid summer afternoon in Hibbing, you can walk into the high school (called by some the most magnificent in the nation), climb the auditorium's stage, and sing to 1,800 empty seats beneath imported Czechoslovakian chandeliers. For years, Mr. Dylan probably rued the day that he sang for his student body, getting pelted on stage. A principal lamented the students' poor behavior, confiding to Jasper's cousin at dinner that evening that "Bob Zimmerman was just trying to sing."

It was three years after Woodstock, Stonewall, and the Greenwich Village encounter that Jas landed in New York on a flight from London. His 15-month absence from the country was now over. That trip had begun on Route 66 in LA and quickly led to Japan—the first of 26 foreign countries.[23] The last thing Jas needed now was more excitement. Before reaching airport customs, he managed to part ways with his flight seatmate, who carried drugs in his mouth. Soon after, however, he stood flat-footed and jaw-dropped as a youth at a subway station yelled, "Hands up!" at a woman, pointing perhaps a pistol barrel at her through his jacket. After a fearful pause, he then added, "Just kidding!" and ran off, disappearing into the city of 7.8 million people.

Still searching for peace and quiet, Jasper poked around fences barricading two buildings under construction. He let himself through a fence gate and in the front door of one building. Finding himself in an elevator and then another that went higher, he pushed the right

[23] See "Around the World in 400 Days" earlier in this book for an account of that trip.

buttons and landed on Floor 100. The elevators he used were just two of the 99 that would later be operational. He walked the perimeter of the floor, with no windows or interior walls yet installed. Jasper was not the first tourist to get an 18-month jump on the opening gun that welcomed John Q. Public into this building. Another intruder had inscribed graffiti on the bare concrete walls of the 100th floor. The graffiti probably survived, though covered over, until the morning of September 11, 2001.

stranger than art itself

On the fifth floor of the Whitney Museum of American Art overlooking the Hudson River, museum guards in spiffy 2016 uniforms have time to survey the 100 works by 83-year-old Frank Stella, one of the greatest living American artists, in the most comprehensive national Stella retrospective ever. They keep their eyes on the fingers of rapt art lovers. And answer questions.

George immigrated to New York City from Ghana with his mother two years ago. He stands uniformed in a corner of one gallery. Jasper walks into that gallery on his first visit to the museum, opened in 2015. He circles one of Stella's works twice. It's called "Raft of the Medusa (Part I)," a multipiece metallic object the size of an extinct mammoth, with its share of molten metal frozen in time. Jasper crouches down for a long minute to investigate. He has an artsy craftsy question for George.

"Why is that one piece of the 'Raft' shaking? It's vibrating like crazy." George examines it and immediately walks into the next gallery. He calls his supervisor Jessie over. They discuss the vibrating component. "It's alive!" Jesse marvels, and leaves to call in other guards. Meanwhile, Jasper points out the enigma to a couple of young women. "It's performance art!" one exclaims.

"Frank Stella visits this retrospective quite often," George tells Jas. "The museum visitors don't know he's among them. He sits on that sofa where you were sitting." Now Jesse comes back with other guards to wonder at the shaking component of the Stella's raft. They leave the gallery. "Jesse is calling the main floor for someone important to come and look," George says.

"Show Frank Stella his vibrating raft the next time he comes," Jas implores George. "Ask Stella if he knows that his work is vibrating, ask him why, and ask him if he planned it."

"No, Frank Stella did not plan this," George answers. "You are the first person who ever noticed it."

Jasper now leaves Floor 5 to examine the work of other artists in the museum, thinking he might have news for the guards to pass on to Georgia O'Keeffe, Jeff Koons, Willem de Kooning, Man Ray, J. Johns, Diane Arbus, Alexander Calder, and Jackson Pollock.

lovably strange to a three-year-old

Jasper, enraptured by art when visiting New York City, never took Art History 101 but thinks he knows good art when he sees it. Especially if it's weird.

Jennifer is a New York City actress who's auditioning for several plays that will premiere in 2016 or 2017. She's at the same museum that Jas is now visiting, the Museum of Modern Art in midtown Manhattan. She's with her husband, who looks of Southeast Asian descent, and their son Alex, who has not yet turned three. Alex needs to be held by his tall father so he can see the art better. Besides, it avoids having the guard call out a warning for Alex to move away from the wall underneath a Gauguin painting so he doesn't poke a painted Polynesian figure in her eye.

Alex is the most vocally avid enthusiast in the museum on this frigid afternoon. He exclaims "I love it!" in front of the creations he sees. His parents ask him "why?" And Alex explains why he loves them.

At Salvador Dali's sculptured "Bust of a Woman" (1933), Alex asks his father why a double ink well and other objects are resting on top of a long baguette balanced on the head of the woman. Jas, standing nearby, doesn't pick up the father's explanation. He is, however, about to explain to Alex and his parents that when this work was first exhibited in 1933, Pablo Picasso's dog is reputed to have eaten the bread. Dali then substituted a plaster baguette for the real one.

Alas, Alex and his family have disappeared, no doubt to see works by Vincent van Gogh, Claes Oldenburg, Gabriel Orozco, Frida Kahlo, and Diego Rivera. It seems probable that some of this art will work its way into Alex's dreams tonight—dreams made of the lovably strange in a large city. As Alex and many a million more fall aslumber, Jasper leaves New York City. He's already aching to return.

The Wildest Month
2012—2020

Next year in the dead of winter, discover the wildest month on earth: New York City's January. I'd suggest spending most of your time at three of the many festivals, while saving a couple hours here and there for museums, a Broadway musical or play, and a morning open rehearsal of the New York Philharmonic Orchestra at Lincoln Center.

Prototype, the premier global festival of opera theater and music theater, celebrates the work of pioneering artists from New York City and around the world. Prototype "is more central to the future of opera with every passing year," notes *The New York Times*. There you'll experience avant-garde opera like never before.

Then spend an evening at North America's most important music industry event, which attracts 1,500 music industry professionals, press corps, and fans like you and me. It's globalFEST's Flagship Festival— 12 acts, three stages, up to a dozen countries.

Don't let Under the Radar—or UTR—slip by. UTR presents cutting-edge performances by artists from the world over who are redefining the act of making theater.

And, if you'll just forego your usual seven or eight hours of sleep, contemporary dance performances at the American Realness festival will keep you awake, as will the Winter Jazz Fest, celebrations of Martin Luther King Jr. at Harlem's Apollo Theater and other venues, the Jewish Film Festival, and coffee at a secret spot on the Lower East Side—the Classic Coffee Shop at 56 Hester Street. If you duck into just one of the city's 3,389 coffee shops, make it this one. Tell Carmine that Jasper, a New York City fan from Minnesota, sent you.

LONDON

Pushing the Boat Out near Heaps of Rubbish
FEBRUARY 6, 2017

Jasper—the traveler in New York City—is now in London. Acquaintances from around the world wonder what he's up to. Friends of acquaintances doubt that he even exists, but he wants all to believe he's real. So, does he take a moment to text you that he's standing in front of the Rosetta Stone in the famed British Museum and has learned that two scientists got all revved up about deciphering hieroglyphs when they saw it? No. Jasper's cell phone is turned off. Besides, it stayed home in North America.

Visiting Westminster Abbey, many who have an iPad would think to send you a photo of the tomb of your favorite queen or king, or the resting place of Chaucer or Browning, Chamberlain or Atlee, Newton or Dickens. Jasper? No. "Dreariest of stones," he argues. You'd think he'd buy you a T-shirt at the Tower of London portraying a heavy block of oak and a gigantic ax used to lop off the heads of perhaps a hundred souls, including royalty. No. "Too macabre," Jasper fears. Macabre or not, Jasper might at least send you a selfie of what a bedraggled Super Bowl fan looks like at 3:25 a.m. (London time) when the game finally ends. No again. Macabre-free it may be, but Jasper is in bed and so bedraggled.

Just when you think Jasper is a make-believe person on a made-up trip, lightning strikes. Jasper wants you to see a photo that leaves him enraptured, venturing to say no one else in the world has it. A question for you: Does the photo show: (a) A pub that hasn't cleaned up the

An eclectic art installation or heaps of rubbish? A diverse group of individuals in London's East End weighed in with opinions. Record your own at this book's website, TomsGlobe.com.

mess on its three outdoor window ledges after a big night, (b) rubbish left by people passing by an abandoned building, or (c) since the street has a number of outdoor wall murals, paintings, and scribbles, an *art installation* created on the outdoor ledges?

Jasper travels down the footpath and importunes waitress Karina in Nude Expresso to explain what the photo shows. He understands her British English, which mixes the accents of London with that of her northern hometown of Newcastle and of Scotland, just over the border from Newcastle. He doesn't quite pick up on some of the other British accents, which she bemusedly relates to him, but both of them are about to howl.

Karina doesn't know the answer to the question about the photo, but she'll go down the Hanbury Street footpath—sidewalk—and have a look in person. In a few days, Jasper will return to Hanbury to check whether Great Britain's best art installation, if that's what this is, still exists. He may also slip into Nude Expresso again.

The final stop for Jasper is the pub at The English Restaurant on nearby Brushfield Street. "What's the most popular of the four draft beers here?" Jasper asks bartender Daniel.

"Paulaner is, but if you're willing to push the boat out, try Neck Oil," Daniel advises.

"Push the WHAT out?!" Jasper exclaims.

"Push the boat out! Be adventurous," the bartender explains.

Without hesitation, Jasper declares, "I will push the boat out!" He orders a half pint. He snaps the only photo ever taken at The English Restaurant in London's East End of a half pint of Neck Oil, next to today's news from *The Guardian* newspaper. He wishes he'd ordered a whole pint. This snapshot, he will send you. If nothing else, he hopes this might once and for all dispel any rumor questioning his very existence or his habitual boat-pushing.

---○---

On Larks in London
FEBRUARY 12, 2017

Last we heard, Jasper had surfaced in East London, fixated by a half pint of Neck Oil and window ledges of rubbish that a perceptive few concluded was a new art installation.

Does Jasper now send us photos taken at the Tate Modern museum of the exhibition of 200 of the photos Elton John has collected, which adorn his Los Angeles home, including the very one that hangs above his bed? No, he does not. Even though Sir Elton's collection of rare vintage prints is one of the greatest private collections on earth. Jasper would've sent a dozen photos of photos, until he read the "Photography Prohibited" sign. "Ironic!" he murmurs to himself.

Does Jasper send a postcard of today's full-scale replica of Shakespeare's thatched-roofed Globe Theater that went up in flames in 1613 during a performance of *Henry the VIII?* No, he does not. And will he give us the lowdown on why he spent the afternoon in a maze of underground bunkers near No. 10 Downing Street? *Why, Yes! Of course he will!*

The entrance sign at the bunkers informs us: "This was the global hub of information on the War, the Government's secret bomb shelter, an easy target that was never hit." One learns, though, that Nazi bombs did destroy over one million homes in London. And that Winston Churchill and an initial staff of eight that grew to 500 mapped out the prosecution of World War II here. And made plans to defend England from a Nazi invasion that a chief staff officer feared might come the very next day, according to a diary early in the war. And from which Churchill addressed his nation, spoke with President Franklin Roosevelt by secure line, and read daily reports from the enigma code-cracking team.

Jasper, often the last person to know something, adds the footnote that he'd always thought the Churchill War Rooms numbered just one or two and were on a second floor with a view. So spending all afternoon in the bunkers was not much, considering that Churchill and his staff were confined here for days on end from 1940 to 1945.

In the evening, Jasper resurfaces in East London after hours in the bunkers. He'd half promised us that he'd return to Hanbury Street to re-observe the rubbish—or art—on three window ledges. Would it be gone, or would someone have enhanced it? When Jasper arrives, four young men are standing in front of the ledges, chatting. They're speaking a foreign language, perhaps Bangladeshi. The trash is still there, a week after Jasper's first visit. "Is this artwork or is this just rubbish?" Jasper asks the four. One by one, the first three say it's rubbish. Then the fourth answers, "Around here you never know. It could be art."

The four then head to a big Bangladeshi supermarket at the corner, filled with cuts of meat and whole fishes, all fresh. The Bangla Cash and Carry will close this year after serving its community for decades, victim of an increase in rent to $500,000 a year in this fast-gentrifying, artsy cool neighborhood. Jasper walks in to buy bananas and realizes he's the only one who does not speak the language.

Back outside, a young German woman walks by the ledges. "What *is* this?" Jasper inquires.

"It is art; if it were rubbish, it would have been removed!" she answers.

Jasper enters the business next door to ask the woman at the counter about *her damn neighbor!* She's never noticed the window ledges, she says, but looking at the photo Jasper took a minute ago, she weighs in. "This is *not* art."

Since Jasper now appears to the casual observer to be taking a poll, he thanks her for her participation and hands her a clipping from *The New York Times.* Jasper cut it out last year at Lost Lake. It's about the place where this woman works, complete with a photo of that business, Librería Bookstore. The bookstore was opened a year ago by an aide to then Prime Minister David Cameron. The article focuses on a new trend in bookstores: a refusal to serve coffee or provide Wi-Fi so that people can read in peace. Jasper can't lug a hardcover book to the countries and continents he's going to next, so he makes note of *The Globe Guide to Shakespeare.* It explains in plain English to an unschooled person such as himself what every one of the Bard's plays means line by line, as well as the works' historical backgrounds.

Going back to Brick Lane, the cross-street half a block away, gentrification has a new, irresistible smell. On the corner is Dark Sugars Chocolates. Jasper orders Cardamom Hot Chocolate for four pounds ($5). The worker picks up her butcher knife and shaves endless amounts of Ghanaian chocolate from two chunks onto her cutting board. Within a few minutes, Jasper is sipping his most favorite hot chocolate ever, while talking to Albanian manager Anduela about the world, including the three window ledges.

"Art is perspective," Anduela explains. "To you, something may be art, to someone else, not. Different people contributed to the items on the three ledges," she opines after looking at Jasper's photos. "Each had their own reason for placing an item there. Some were drunk. Some found a handy place to leave their trash. And Jasper, when you place your Dark Sugars paper cup on the ledge like you say you will, you'll have your own reason for setting it there."

Today, Jasper's Dark Sugars cup imprinted with his fingerprints and lip smudges is indeed artistically resting on one of the window ledges, placed there by Jasper for his own reason: "Enhancing what he has named 'Great Britain's Newest and Most Endearing Pop Art Exhibit.'"

A certain well-known artist might appreciate the window ledges as much as our Jasper, who is the namesake of Jasper Johns, an 86-year-old American painter and sculptor who, Wikipedia says, is associated with "Abstract Expressionism, Neo-Dada, and Pop Art." Our Jasper is into the Abstract and Pop parts. The Neo-Dada, not so much.

As Jasper walks the 10 blocks back to the Aldgate East "underground"—subway—he surmises that the window ledges belonged to a Bangladeshi rock or punk club that left the lights on when it went defunct. Over weeks or months, passersby such as himself have left their marks, some firmly believing this *is* an art installation, while others disposed of their rubbish or were just drunk. Glancing at other photos on this book's website will prove Jasper is not a fake namesake making fake claims of going on larks in East London, West London, and all around town.

HOMEBOUND

Minnesota: Almost Home

My friend Dan MacMeekin has been a major inspiration for everything I've written. Why, you ask? Because he encouraged me to write as I traveled and sent me comments from readers to whom he'd routed my writings. This account responds to a question from his cousin.

APRIL 23, 2016

To Dan from Bogotá's Environs:

Your Michigan cousin asked: "Does Tom like Minnesota as much as the places he visits?" That got me to thinking.

Thinking and imprinting in my head . . . Living on or near the Mesabi Iron Range are great cousins and friends I've known since age three or four, or just since 1970 or 2010. A brother, sister, and others come back to visit for class reunions, the unequaled 4th of July celebrations, and the December Weihnachtsfest in Biwabik. I go door to door in a few Range towns for the Democratic-Farmer-Labor (DFL) candidates. Barack Obama carried my nearly all-white hometown of Biwabik with 70% of the vote in the last two presidential elections.

Most summer evenings, packing a salad and newspaper, I paddle my kayak a few minutes across the lake. Upon lazy completion of my dual project, I brush remaining bits of salad off the plate into the lake. I watch multiple bluish explosions, most time-delayed, from just a smidgeon of oil. Miniscule, triangle-shaped floating remnants of spinach propel themselves with their own residue of oil in majestic figure-eight movements and sudden lefts, rights, and U-turns. I also observe what insects, loons, and eagles do, though they don't yet notice that I'm on the slippery slope to debasing the water.

From September to Christmas, celebrations come one after another, affording us ethnic foods from European immigrant times of (just) 100 to 120 years ago. The women of the historic Kaleva Hall in the city of Virginia present a feast for the eyes, ears, and taste buds in a one-day Christmas Bazaar—I load up on the famed Finnish cardamom biscuit, sweet breads, homemade candies, Kaleva-branded coffee, and ethnic lunches before heading 200 miles south to share the treasure with my farm friends and with 103-year-old cousin Alice and her daughter.

The Nelimark Homestead Museum in Embarrass is often open for coffee, the purchase of Finnish breads, local jams and pickles, and visits inside century-old log buildings. At Nelimark in June, the Sisu Heritage organization of Embarrass hosts National Sauna Day—a holiday Sisu created. Drive with your lights off through the remote forest cemetery in this same rural community one Saturday night in December: a hundred candles burn inside a hundred partly hollowed-out cylinders of ice—a Finnish tradition.

I changed my travel schedule just now to make it home by the first Friday in May for the monthly Aamu Kaffit (Morning Coffee) in the 100% rural community of Palo, a few miles from my home. Aamu Kaffit is a name that doesn't do the event justice, because friends and strangers are treated to a Finnish baked egg dish, homemade pies of many kinds, and assorted add-ons. The 60 to 80 who gather even before the opening hour at the Loon Lake Community Center don't leave anytime soon. Aamu Kaffit is spearheaded by Vivian Williams and her daughter Beth Wilkes, Palo natives. All proceeds go to supporting the survival of the community center, built in the 1950s as the marvelous Palo-Markham School.

A winter celebration that has put these school grounds on the map for four generations of Minnesotans is the Finnish Sliding Festival, or Laskiainen, an event like no other in the United States. Sit down on a wooden seat and take several hair-raising spins on the *vipukelkka* (whip sled), pushed 'round and 'round a central anchoring post by slip-sliding festival goers, since a sheet of ice covers the ground. Or sled down the steep hill a few feet away and come to a rest on frozen Loon Lake. Hike back up and do it again, at least if you're a child.

A wild concert is performed each summer at the same Palo venue by a farm boy who won a full scholarship to study opera singing at Rowan University in New Jersey. The concert has a new title each year, like *Steve Solkela's Overpopulated One-Man Band* and *Solkelamania*. Steve's talents as a lyricist and songwriter are evident in the new CD he releases every year, his Solkela.com postings, and his YouTube music videos. Steve makes an appearance earlier in "Tales of Strange in a Large City." In that New York City story, though, Steve goes under the name Mikko Aarila, one of several characters he manufactured in high school for a hilarious solo competition in declamation (while I manufactured the name Jasper for myself for no apparent reason).

In Markham—Palo's neighbor—you don't need an invitation to walk into the log home built by Eli Wirtanen. The Finnish immigrant homesteaded 40 acres of beautiful forest in 1904 and hard-scrabbled together a farm, now known as the Wirtanen Pioneer Farm. Citizens have preserved the house, sauna, and other log buildings. On any given day, you may be all alone at the secluded farm on rolling hills for as long as you desire. Travel to the farm for the fall festival in September, though, and mill among crafters, artisans, authors, and musicians.

Visit the Vermilion Iron Range and a wonderful Native American museum at the Bois Forte Indian Reservation, next to the one-thousand-mile shoreline of Lake Vermilion. A few miles away, descend in an industrial-strength elevator to 689 feet below sea level. Step out into the old Soudan underground iron mine. Don't panic. You'll still be 723 feet higher than the surface of the Dead Sea—the lowest place on earth at minus 1,412 feet.

You might also tour the gamma ray lab on another deep level of the mine. All right, I think it's the cosmic ray that's involved along with a gaggle of neutrinos. The lab won't stay open for an eternity, though, so phone the physicists quick if you see any of these bounding or bonding around your homestead. You'll help them win a Nobel Prize in origin of the universe. When the physicists leave, the lab will certainly open up every summer for science tours "of the deep."

In July, thousands enjoy the Northern Lights Music Festival, a renowned three-week classical music and opera fest with student and professional talent from several countries. Its founding artistic director is Aurora native Veda Zuponcic, an internationally acclaimed pianist and Rowan University Professor of Music.

The Iron Range is home not only to the below-sea-level Soudan iron mine and above-sea-level splendid lakes, but also to several hundred miles of snowmobile and bicycle trails, as well as skiing and golfing at Giant's Ridge. Not to mention outstanding schools and colleges, public libraries, historical centers, the Mesabi Family YMCA, United Way, and health facilities, including the Range Mental Health Center. It's also home to the hometowns of Mikko Aarilla / Steve Solkela, Bob Dylan, Kevin McHale, and Vincent Bugliosi.

And Biwabik is the hometown of Megan Marsnik, author of *Under Ground*, an Iron Range novel that tells the spellbinding tale of brutally exploited immigrant mine workers a century ago. Our state paper, the *Star Tribune*, first serialized the novel, which is told from the perspective of an immigrant woman, Katva Kovich. Also a native of Biwabik is Jerry Pushcar, whose book *Waters Beneath My Feet* recounts a journey over unimaginable obstacles paddling his canoe from New Orleans to Alaska.

The Land of the Loon Festival welcomes summer and thousands of visitors to the city of Virginia. The Lyric Center for the Arts in this Queen City of the North treats everyone with don't-miss live music and theater performances—and fine arts exhibits, too. In nearby Eveleth, the United States Hockey Hall of Fame sits atop a hill, and the world's biggest hockey stick is unmistakable on the main street.

Anchoring the center of the 100-mile-long Iron Range are Hibbing and Chisholm. Chisholm is home to the Minnesota Discovery Center and the Minnesota Museum of Mining. On the edge of Hibbing, above one of the world's largest open pit mines, watch trucks two stories high and supersized electric shovels at work. And for music fans, a dotted line like no other was drawn from Hibbing to Manhattan a couple dozen pages ago in "Tales of Strange in a Large City."

Please don't forget Grand Rapids—hometown of Judy Garland—and Ely at the other extreme of the Iron Range—gateway to the out-of-this-world motor-free Boundary Waters Canoe Area Wilderness, with its 1,200 pristine lakes and 1,200 miles of canoe routes.

As in cultures all over the world, the festivals, outdoor opportunities, and musical and dramatical enlightenment that I've mentioned exist only because members of the community volunteer their time, knowledge, and enthusiasm.

Now I'll zip through the mountains to Bogotá and get home by the first Friday in May to start another round of the irresistible. Dan, please thank your cousin for making me think anew about where I live. Tell her I am almost home, and that yes, I do like Minnesota as much as the places I visit.

Tom

The Ancient Haymakers
AUGUST 17, 2011

the haymaker's prologue
My friends Craig and Vicky Trytten run a farm 300 miles to the south, hard by the Iowa border. In early spring, Craig fell on ice outside the pig barn and broke his leg. Now it's summer, and hay must be made. "Come here and sit on a tractor!" Craig pleads on the telephone.

I know the place. Farm-fresh milk three meals a day. Organic hamburger from a pasture-fed Black Angus that roamed the hills without the debilitating effects of that alien food, corn. Pork chops from the pig barn where the animals are fed oats, slop, and skim milk left over after nearby Amish farmers have churned butter by hand. Eggs from the Amish, too, and their loaves of bread just out of the wood-burning oven in a hardwood-floor kitchen crisscrossed by several pair of bare feet, topped by children under the age of 10. That Amish farm not miles away also sells greeting cards handwritten and colored by 18-year-old Lovina, blueberry jam, pickled beets, and home-made grape nuts cereal. It sits among rolling gravel roads without power poles, all taken down by the power company since the Amish have no use for electricity.

Taking care of your cows is ancient stuff—the Egyptians did it daily 8,000 years ago. I'm thinking they did it in Asia, where my father's father's father to the nth degree lived at the time—this according to a National Geographic analysis of swabs from my mouth. Making hay is as old as dirt, too, one might surmise. It may have been done in my family for 3,000 years, I feel, save for the last 60. I'll reconnect with 150 generations before me but cheat and ride a tractor that pulls imple-ments like a scythe, tedder, and raker.

Wait! Choosing wisdom over a rash decision to sit on a tractor, I ask Roy Coombe, my newspaper boss from my high school days who is now 86 years old: "Roy, can an old guy like me sit on a tractor?"

His fist slams down on the table. "You can learn!" he booms.

With his billowing words bouncing around in my head, I ride my motorcycle south. Oh, the Glorious Days of Summer are now here!

the haying operation

Hold your horses! What we've got here is a juggling act. Two tractors are down—one spraying hydraulic fluid all over hell, and the other having a fit inside an axle and sent out of state to the John Deere Doctor of Decorah. The round bailer has a broken belt, so the Spee-Dee Delivery truck will have to hurry over with a new one. The power take-off shaft on the rotary scythe keeps spinning, but the connecting chain that turns the grass cutters has stopped.

Move the electric fences every day so the beef cattle and milk cows find fresh fields. Don't touch a hot wire or you'll have a surprised look on your face like a heifer. Don't stumble over rusty barbed wire hiding in tall weeds. Corral the calves with pink eye into ever narrower pens. Don't blink or you'll miss seeing the visiting vet needle penicillin into the calves' eyes. Collar a calf that jumps over a half door and out of the barn. Catch the house dog that escapes outside and is chasing everything that moves. Get inside and eat supper at eight, two hours earlier than the night before.

Now quit veering off the windrow of hay in front of your tractor. And quit blaming it on your transfixed eyes staring back over your shoulder out the rear window, in full-blown admiration of the work you've done. Remember next time to shift into the best gear of the eight to drive down the slippery slope to the lower pasture so you don't lock your brakes and slide there willy-nilly. Now we've got rows of cut hay that get wetter with each damned drop of rain. We're looking up at all the balls we're juggling in the air. If one drops, forget it. Plenty more have to stay up, knowing all the while that we'll be up shit creek if it rains yet again. Keep our eyes on the balls flying, not down at the rusty barbed wire scratches on my leg or Craig's infected toe, and hope his broken leg holds out for the duration.

At last, alas, it's over. Now I'm trying to séance to my ancestors of thousands of years ago. I expect to be charmed by their recounted highlights of making hay during one ancient midsummer week. I'll let you know.

A Brief History of Traveling Genes

Will new discoveries refine or even upend some of what we believed this morning? Most certainly, so our minds should be willing to self-tune with each new bit of knowledge for as long as we live.

How did my ancestors get to America from Africa over the last 60,000 years? Current history does tell us that Paavo Pyrro emigrated from Finland in 1892 and settled in Biwabik, Minnesota, as Paul Mattson, his name changed by a tongue-twisted foreman in Massachusetts, where Paul first worked. He married Finnish immigrant Matilda Launola. Together they had children George (my father), Arvid, Tenie, Aune, and Ernie, and another three who died in infancy. They built a small home on the edge of town and benefitted from a sauna, garden, cow, and creek outside. To the north lay only an iron mine and endless forests crossed by native trails all the way to Hudson Bay.

But what about my grandfather Paul's father? And his father's father, and all the fathers before that? To reveal my deep ancestry, I swabbed DNA from my mouth and mailed it to the Genographic Project, a world history–making endeavor of National Geographic and IBM. As far back as 200,000 to 300,000 years ago, humans who were physically the same as us were thriving. They're often called "modern humans"—short for anatomically modern humans (AMH), also known as Homo sapiens—and are distinguished from now extinct archaic humans such as Neanderthals. Almost all modern humans' family lineages died out over time, but my own ancestry and that of every human alive today can be traced to a female who lived 150,000 to 200,000 years ago in Africa. She's been dubbed "Mitochondrial Eve." Other females were alive back then, but eventually, each of their lineages stopped having further offspring.

All humans alive today also descended from a man who lived in Africa between 150,000 and 300,000 years ago, dubbed "Y-chromosome Adam." He was the only male whose lineage is still around today.

Homo sapiens' intellectual capacity began developing in leaps and bounds around 75,000 years ago. The reason may lie in the emergence of language. Specific genetic mutations that occurred in humans may have allowed the brain to develop its capacity for languages.[24] The genetic alterations did not occur in chimpanzees, and chimps are therefore not born with the circuitry for speech and language.

Language eventually gave modern humans a nice advantage over other human species. The modern humans of the time could better plan ahead, cooperate with one another, develop improved tools and weapons, exploit resources, and replace other hominids, such as the Neanderthals and Denisovans, whom modern humans encountered in Eurasia after leaving Africa.

You could've written on the back of a postage stamp all that any Homo sapiens knew about Denisovans between about 40,000 years ago (when they disappeared) and 2010. In that telling year, Homo sapiens scientists excavating the Denisova Cave in Siberia discovered a fossilized finger bone that genetic analysis proved was from a previously unknown human species, which was named "Homo denisova." The Denisovans and Neanderthals were just two of several human species that made the world their home "at one and the same time" for about two million years until quite recently—about 40,000 years ago for Neanderthals and Denisovans, and perhaps 50,000 years ago in the case of Homo floresiensis, who lived on Flores Island in today's Indonesia. When ocean levels rose, these islanders were trapped. Big people, who require more food to survive, died first on this resource-poor island, while smaller ones survived much better. Over time, they became dwarves, as did an elephant species.[25]

The Homo sapiens' replacement of the other hominids did not come without intimate personal contact. I'm about 2.6% Neanderthal

---

[24] Nicholas Wade, "Speech Gene Shows It's Bossy Nature," *New York Times,* November 11, 2009.

[25] Yuval Noah Harari, *Sapiens—A Brief History of Mankind* (New York: Harper Perennial, 2015), 5–8,

and 2.2% Denisovan—about the same amount as many other people in the modern Middle East, Europe, and Americas. People from Sub-Saharan Africa, where there was no such contact, do not carry those genes. (Up to 6% of the DNA of modern Melanesians and Aboriginal Australians is Denisovan DNA.)

Having lived in the same Eurasian regions for thousands of years, perhaps thousands of individuals were half Neanderthal and half modern human, including one or more ancestors of many of us. What was said about the hybrids in Neanderthal and modern human communities? Or, if lacking language, what was believed? Were hybrids accepted, rejected, admired, or stereotyped?

If I could go back in time and meet one of my ancient ancestors for a week, would I pick one who was half modern human and half Neanderthal? And how would I answer a follow-up question: "Since two such persons happen to fit the bill for your lineage, do you pick the hybrid raised in a Neanderthal community or the one from a nearby Homo sapiens community?" That's a tough one to answer. But I'd hope the one I do pick happens to be hanging out with the other one that week. I'd suggest, "Let's all go foraging and hunting, and you can show me how y'all do it"—as I tie my Adidas running shoe laces tighter.

The Neanderthals, we've recently learned, used tools and cared for the elderly and infirm. They were stronger and faster than our Homo sapiens ancestors. Much more than Neanderthals, our Homo sapiens ancestors were "mad" for exploring and settling continents and specks of land in the oceans. While Neanderthals lived sustainably in harmony with their environment, Homo sapiens "have managed to get the planet to a point where it's in danger" in just a quarter of the time that Neanderthals lived.[26]

My ancestors, too, succumbed to this typical Homo sapiens wanderlust. About 70,000 years ago, an early man in my patrilineal lineage

---

[26] *Neanderthal*, a PBS television series, February 18, 2018.

(my father's father's father to the nth degree) was living in northeastern Africa, probably present-day Ethiopia, Kenya, or Tanzania. My direct patrilineal ancestors left Africa about 60,000 years ago, perhaps rafting across the narrow strait at the southern end of the Red Sea between Africa and present-day Yemen.

The first 35,000 years were relatively slow moving for that lineage. They made their way through Southwest and then South and East Asia, apparently traversing today's Iraq, Iran, Afghanistan, northern bits of Pakistan and India, the Plateau of Tibet north of Mount Everest, and China. They possibly lived for generations within 100 or 200 miles of today's Beijing.

By 15,000 years ago, they had swung northwest, crossed Mongolia, and faced the rugged conditions of Siberia. By 10,000 years ago, they were one of the few descendent lines to survive Siberia. They moved west across present-day Russia and eventually settled in Finland.

My direct matrilineal ancestors, on the other hand, did not make that 12,000-mile detour to the Far East and back. Instead, like the matrilineal lineage of my Biwabik friend Eddie and the patrilineal lineage of my cousin Marvin, they meandered north and northwest toward Finland for over 50,000 years, after crossing from Africa. They traversed present-day Saudi Arabia, Turkey, and Central Europe.

In 1900, my mother's mother Sanna and her husband Johan Puskanen migrated from Finland to Chisholm in northern Minnesota. This migratory route proved spectacularly fortuitous for my sister Mary, brother James, and me. Why? Because 40 years later, the Puskanens' daughter Elmy met George Mattson at the log cabin of Elmy's sister, when George visited Cedar Island Lake near Biwabik as a tax assessor. They would marry and have three children. Migrations have lasting consequences!

My mother told me a few times that when I was a bare handful of years old, I exclaimed, feeling wonderful after a warm bath, "I'm so happy I was born, but I feel so sorry for all those who weren't born." She asked me over the years what I was thinking. "Maybe I was thinking

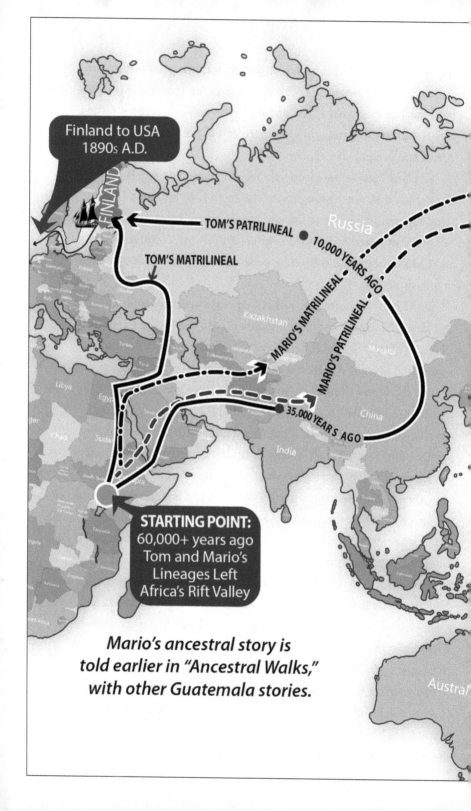

Finland to USA
1890s A.D.

FINLAND

TOM'S PATRILINEAL

Russia

10,000 YEARS AGO

TOM'S MATRILINEAL

MARIO'S MATRILINEAL

Kazakhstan

MARIO'S PATRILINEAL

Mongolia

China

35,000 YEARS AGO

India

STARTING POINT:
60,000+ years ago
Tom and Mario's
Lineages Left
Africa's Rift Valley

*Mario's ancestral story is
told earlier in "Ancestral Walks,"
with other Guatemala stories.*

Australi

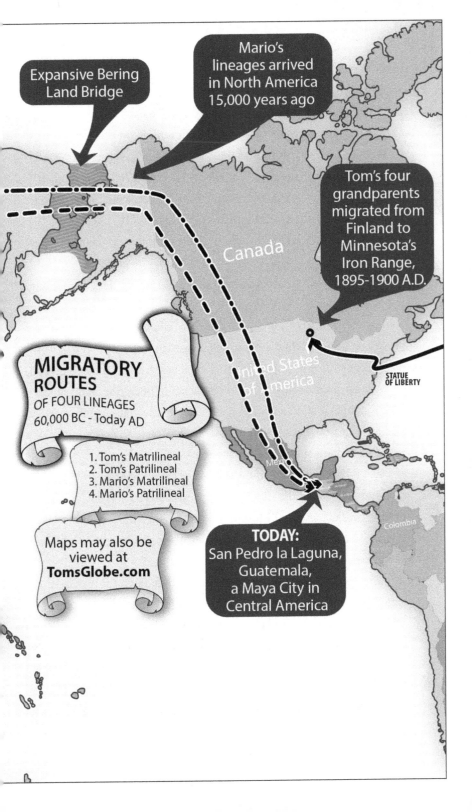

Expansive Bering Land Bridge

Mario's lineages arrived in North America 15,000 years ago

Tom's four grandparents migrated from Finland to Minnesota's Iron Range, 1895-1900 A.D.

Canada

STATUE OF LIBERTY

MIGRATORY ROUTES
OF FOUR LINEAGES
60,000 BC - Today AD

1. Tom's Matrilineal
2. Tom's Patrilineal
3. Mario's Matrilineal
4. Mario's Patrilineal

Maps may also be viewed at **TomsGlobe.com**

United States of America

Mexico

Colombia

TODAY:
San Pedro la Laguna, Guatemala, a Maya City in Central America

that life is so fantastic and miraculous that most potential births don't happen, and they're just for the lucky few," I answered.

Roy Rivers recently recalled that 80 years ago, when he was a boy and a Mattson neighbor, Grandma Matilda Mattson opened the sauna on Wednesday and Saturday nights to neighbors, charging a dime each —and I remember she served coffee and dessert in the tiny kitchen for that dime. The sauna-goers came into the house before and after the sauna, speaking much Finnish.

"Roy," I asked, "did the neighbor Sherek family and their kids come to sauna?"

"Yes," he said, "they sometimes did, and they preferred bartering to paying dimes."

Mother Francis Sherek, Roy said, sent a son out with a wooden bucket on Sundays, first ringing the inside top with lard. The boy— perhaps one known to all as Moon, Pye, Blackie, Pete, Chops, Pinhead, or Susie—would come home with a bucket of beer, not foaming too much, thanks to the lard. "The Shereks and Slovenian friends partied Sunday afternoons out in their yard. They danced to polka music. We could hear them singing," Roy told me.

Just a few years ago, Louie, the last of the 13 Sherek siblings, died past age 90. At the funeral, the priest let us know that "the last of the Shereks has died." I found it curious, since the front pews were filled with Sherek grandchildren and great-grandchildren. I held back a chuckle.

The Sherek DNA will probably be handed down for hundreds of generations more, all because Francis and John Sherek somewhere, somehow, met and raised children. The Shereks and Mattsons of the 21st century still know each other—not to mention other early Biwabik families like the Licaris, Setnickers, Newtons, Holmstroms, Anzelcs, Hendersons, Nopolas, and Dewhursts—all because of the somewheres and somehows of human life. Over the decades, many other energetic families have moved to Iron Range towns, helping revitalize them, just as in communities around the world over the long expanse of time.

NOTES IN BOTTLES

UNREMEMBERED REMEMBRANCES

Last night, I dreamt that I folded up a story, stuck it in a bottle, corked it, and tossed it in the ocean. It was so mesmerizing to watch it drift away into near-certain oblivion that I did it again. The tosses eventually turned into dozens. Each bottle and cork were of different styles, and the seas numbered seven. I'd scribbled my hometown of Biwabik, Minnesota, on the notes, sometimes adding the post office box. I jotted down in a tattered notebook into which of the seven seas I threw each note.

Then an envelope sent from afar appeared at my doorstep with the mailman. I first studied the postmark and sender's address on the envelope: my bottle thrown in the South Pacific was found in England! Inside, I found words in my handwriting, unremembered remembrances. Then another worn message appeared, having traveled halfway around the world, and later others arrived. Since a dream sent me dormant words about six real experiences in my life, I am passing them on to someone special: *you.*

• • •

Called "one of the greatest railway journeys on earth," I was on it somewhere in Southern Peru moving toward Bolivia. At a nondescript stop, word came to me that I could get off, walk forward, and climb into the locomotive. Once inside the locomotive and moving again,

I signaled subtly to the engineer that I wanted to sit where he was sitting. He obliged. There I was, driving the locomotive, pulling a train full of passengers. By and by, it occurred to me that if I got us into a wreck, I'd have a lot of explaining to do. And Exhibit No. 1 in official proceedings might just be the video the engineer shot of me at the controls. So I stood up and stepped back. The engineer, who was licensed to replace me, took over. Safety was no longer my responsibility.

● ● ●

Bums used to ride the American rails for years and live as communities in track-side huts. The banging of pots and pans, the stories told at all hours, the heat, the cold, the railroad police, they would not be for me, unless beyond choice it was a life I lived in the Depression-era 1930s. Borrowed nostalgia, though, drifted above my head in Miss Carol Maxwell's 10th-grade American literature class, as we read a Carl Sandburg poem about his life as a hobo in the late 1890s. The same nostalgia enveloped my thoughts six years later, when I was about to make my way by hook or crook from my Uncle Buzz and Aunt Jeanette's family home near Santa Rosa, California, to Bakersfield, 330 miles to the south, and then east to Phoenix and Dallas.

I phoned a small railroad stop, inquiring when the next day's freight train would come through. The man told me the time, emphasizing, "You have to get your freight here an hour early." Before departure time, after a ride to the station from my Uncle Buzz, my head was nervously turning 90 degrees left and right as I grabbed the ladder on a boxcar. I climbed atop, engulfed with unimaginable anticipation of my 330 miles riding the rails.

No one saw me, and my ride was off to a charming start, I thought. "Hey, mate," a sharp voice yelled up to me within a minute. "Hey, mate," it came again. I stayed silent. "Hey, mate!" Eventually I sheepishly peeked over the edge toward the ground. "Come down here!"

My new railroad friend—I think he was the brakeman—invited me to jump in the caboose with him. "Lay down on the bench every time we go by a station." He offered me a Snicker's bar, fresh from a vending machine. Unbelievably, my railway companion turned out to be a classmate of my 10th-grade teacher Carol Maxwell at Fairfield High in Iowa. I didn't mention the Carl Sandburg poem from Ms. Maxwell's class that put me on the road to riding rails. I don't think I mentioned that Ms. Maxwell, upon her arrival in Minnesota's iron mining towns fresh out of college, expected to see townsfolk walking on wooden sidewalks and us teenage boys strutting about with a pack of cigarettes twisted into a sleeve of our T-shirts, right on our mining-country biceps.

The train moved on, though, and I was now enjoying the California sunshine from atop a boxcar, belting out an impromptu campaign speech for my *Biwabik Times* boss Roy Coombe, who was running for the state legislature back home. It's the only campaign speech I ever gave. It was a real barnburner, but no one heard it.

As dusk settled into darkness, I found my way inside a boxcar to get a roof over my head. Good thing Uncle Buzz had given me a well-worn sweater that I believe dated back to the 1930s. And newspapers, too. "Layer them over you when it gets cold," Uncle Buzz had said. He would know, having hopped freight cars with a friend from Chisholm, Minnesota, to Chicago to see the 1933 Century of Progress Exposition—really a World's Fair. They gained free admission by yanking up the perimeter fence and sliding under. Uncle Buzz and his sister, my Aunt Lil, were amazed to run into each other. Neither had known that the other was there.

I wasn't all by my lonesome inside the boxcar that night in California. Another bum settled in at the other end. My brother James had advised, "Take enough to drink and don't fall asleep among strangers." Thirsty and in the dark, my fingers found a steel wall grating to pry open my glass bottle of Coke. The metal cap popped off and bounced down the floor in the darkness toward my fellow traveler.

I thought I'd better offer to share the refreshment with him. He was an African American from the Deep South, and I could just make out his answer: "Oh, no," he said. "I thought you were throwing rocks at me." Having cleared the air, I think we both slept well.

When I woke at daybreak, he was gone. Through the open boxcar door, I saw a ship-shape company of kids my age standing erect in a nearby training field: they were US Army recruits for the Vietnam War. I had arrived in Oakland, California. I was hungry. Luckily, a café was open for breakfast at 6 a.m. Back on the rails, I headed to Southern California.

At daybreak the next morning, I was thirsty and dirty. The train was at a dead standstill. I maneuvered myself out of the boxcar onto the ground. A motel lady unlocked her office door and handed me a glass of water. I took a snooze under her palm tree before hitchhiking out of state with a motorist who implied he was some low-level fugitive. I traveled with him for a thousand miles. By the time I got to Phoenix after 500 miles, though, the rails were history, and I was committed to automobiles. Except at the end, when I was in a junky pickup truck with a grandfather and grandson in Dallas. That night, they were stopped by the police just past the Texas School Book Depository for a burned-out taillight. It was the first time I felt bad for anybody in many a mile.

It's a surprise, isn't it, how well some notes weather their journey in a bottle?

• • •

I have a hard spot in my heart for La Ocho, the old downtown Tijuana jail. It was there that a Mexican-American (in Tijuana for a wedding party), three youthful US Navy seamen (supposed to be spending the night in San Diego on their nuclear submarine), an unknown soul (who never said a word), and I were crowded together in an ice-cold . . .

Hold on a second, I just read better news. The *Los Angeles Times* reported (in 2010): *Notorious Tijuana Jail to be Just a Dark Memory.* "If the walls of this Mexican jail could talk," the article read, "they would curse in Spanish, and English. Decades ago, when Americans visited in hard-partying hordes, more than a few drunk sailors and bar patrons ended up in one of these dank fetid cages," steps away from drug kingpins and assassins in the same cellblock.

Well, my cellmates and I were locked up on that raucous Saturday night filled with Mexican songs for transgressions like . . . (Regrettably, the remainder of this note in a bottle was rendered nearly illegible by saltwater from one or all of those seven seas. If I'm able to add more, you'll be the first to know.)

● ● ●

We hung around for a few days in a small Columbian city, my new friend Juan Jose and me. He'd fled there from the only place he'd ever known: Bogotá. For a couple years, no one knew where he was— not his family, not his friends, not his enemies. It would have been dangerous any other way.

He found himself running down Bogotá streets, he told me late one night, away from men on motorcycles intent on killing him. Just minutes before, there'd been a knock on his upper-floor apartment door. He dreaded knocks. He squeezed out the kitchen window and climbed to the roof. He was pursued roof to high-rise roof by those who'd knocked and entered. Then he was on the ground, running still. He escaped. That's when he fled Bogotá forever.

One night, a week before the spine-chilling knocks on his door, Juan Jose had visited with an acquaintance in a dark alley. The acquaintance (let's say "associate") was not happy with him. Indeed, he was so unhappy that he jammed the barrel of a loaded handgun deep into Juan's mouth. Juan listened as the associate counted down the seconds

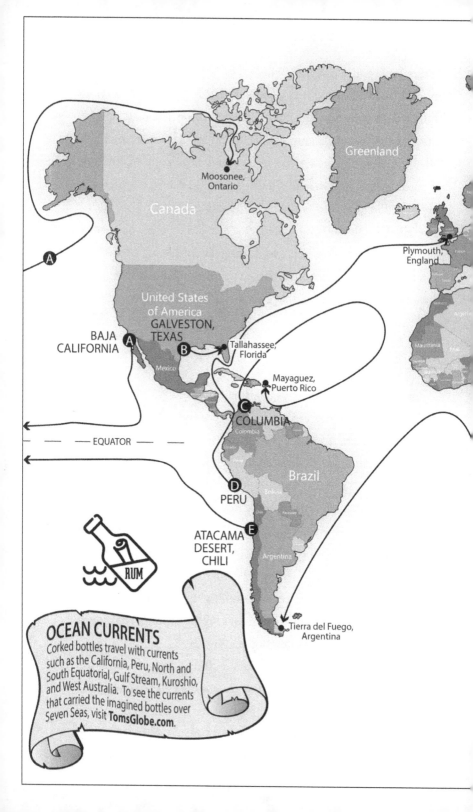

Greenland

Moosonee,
Ontario

Canada

Plymouth,
England

United States
of America
GALVESTON,
TEXAS

BAJA
CALIFORNIA

Ⓐ

Ⓑ Tallahassee,
Florida

Mayaguez,
Puerto Rico

Mexico

Ⓒ
COLUMBIA

Colombia

Brazil

— EQUATOR —

Ⓓ
PERU

ATACAMA
DESERT,
CHILI

Ⓔ

Argentina

RUM

Tierra del Fuego,
Argentina

OCEAN CURRENTS

Corked bottles travel with currents such as the California, Peru, North and South Equatorial, Gulf Stream, Kuroshio, and West Australia. To see the currents that carried the imagined bottles over Seven Seas, visit **TomsGlobe.com**.

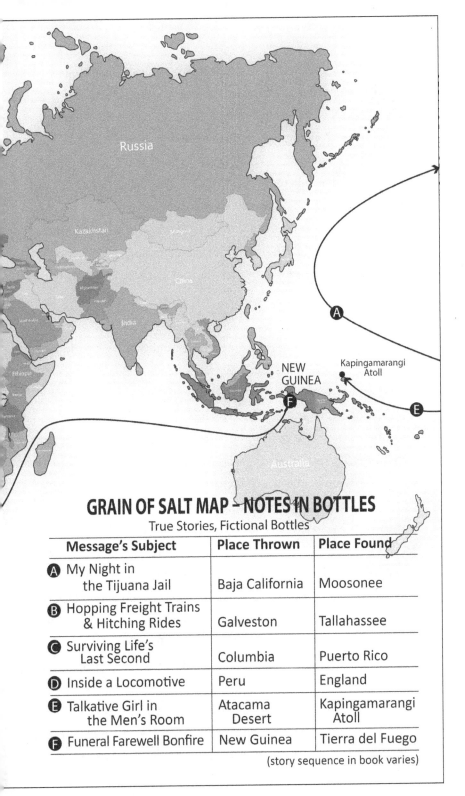

GRAIN OF SALT MAP – NOTES IN BOTTLES
True Stories, Fictional Bottles

Message's Subject	Place Thrown	Place Found
A My Night in the Tijuana Jail	Baja California	Moosonee
B Hopping Freight Trains & Hitching Rides	Galveston	Tallahassee
C Surviving Life's Last Second	Columbia	Puerto Rico
D Inside a Locomotive	Peru	England
E Talkative Girl in the Men's Room	Atacama Desert	Kapingamarangi Atoll
F Funeral Farewell Bonfire	New Guinea	Tierra del Fuego

(story sequence in book varies)

he still had to live: "3, 2, 1." At that moment, a friend of Juan's appeared out of nowhere. He had a loaded firearm too, and pulled the trigger. The bullet killed the man holding a gun in Juan's mouth before he could count from one to zero. Juan fell to the ground, stunned. His friend screamed at him to jump up and run or they'd both be dead. The man with a bullet hole in his head had brothers. That is why Juan dreaded knocks on his door, he confided to me.

Juan has never returned to Bogotá. He's now married and the father of a daughter. He visits with his mother, sisters, and cousins on social media. As for his father, he was shot and killed in Medellin.

• • •

My stay in Bolivia is nearing the end. I must decide what to do next. I have to save time for a four-hour mountain bike ride down the "World's Most Dangerous Road." I thus make the time, discovering that the road descends from 15,050 to 3,500 feet. Each year, one or two hundred people go over the cliffs and turn up dead; almost all are in vehicles. A couple years ago, however, a young French woman flew off the road on her bicycle in sketchy circumstances. The road isn't always wide enough for a descending bicyclist to meet an oncoming truck. Cyclists have to dismount and stand erect, the drop-off inches behind their heels. We survivors and our rented bikes are eventually trucked from Coroico in the steaming lowlands back up to 15,050 feet, and then to La Paz, the world's highest seat of government at 11,975 feet.

For my last precious hours in the country, I imagine I'm spending the night in a museum. A blackened room's 40 small spotlights each shine on a different wondrous mask used in ceremonies from one end of the country to the other. I leave the eerie room at long last, remembering now that I *am* in a museum. Other galleries display 167 Bolivian weavings, some new and some from 200 A.D., worn by people over a thousand years before the Inca culture existed.

I didn't make just one trip to the men's room, but three, each with my digital camera in video mode. I captured the teenage girl spilling her aching heart from a TV screen above the urinal. She has "zits, zits, zits, zits," she's not pregnant (yet), her boyfriend is on her case, it's so hard to be a woman, and she may live for only one more month (in Spanish, with English subtitles).

You want to let her rest her heavy head on your shoulder because her presence seems so real. You realize the TV screen portrays her as if in the adjoining room, looking at you through an opening. A moment of study reveals that her setting is the women's restroom. She then gets up and flushes her toilet. Every urinal user is treated to this avant-garde Argentinian-Italian performance art.

Such is the Museum of Ethnography and Folklore in La Paz, Bolivia. The curators for folklore and ethnography—the study and recording of human cultures—were apparently just fine with putting a talkative teenage girl in the men's room.

Racing nearly out of control down the world's most dangerous road and ensconced for a night in a museum and its men's room took all the time I had left to spend in Colombia. Save for making it to the continent's Caribbean shore to toss out a bottle with this note into uncertain waters. With the expectation that the words would never again be seen as ink on a page.

• • •

Head for the middle of New Guinea if "remote" feels like a good place for you. Invite yourself as I did into the cockpit of the jet flying high above the island. The green mountains below look beyond wonderful —left, right, and center—and the lower the plane flies during descent, the faster the planet seems to go. I made just one mistake in the cockpit: I asked if I should leave now. "You can," the pilot said. I exited, and to this day wonder if I could've stayed and helped the jet land, or at least seen how it's done. I won't ever know. I don't have the flight number or the pilot's name, and I'll keep the airline's identity under wraps.

Minutes after touching down on the airstrip in Wamena, Irian Jaya, Indonesia, a young man approached me. Jos Awom, my newfound friend, hiking companion, and guide became visibly excited a couple days later. For hours, we'd been on trails that native inhabitants had been using for thousands of years. A few words mentioned by a passerby triggered my guide to cross one of the many fantastical wooden foot bridges—each one-of-a-kind in the world. The local people have probably designed and constructed such bridges for a hundred generations. No outsider ever saw any bridge or anyone from this valley until 1938, when explorers met a Dani tribe.

These trails and more stream-spanning bridges took Jos and me at an ever faster clip to the edge of a village square filled with people ceremonializing—*what*, I did not know. Jos said nothing to me. We stood with a few other nonvillagers just outside the town square's rough-hewn perimeter fence of logs and branches, all welcome to that point.

A mound of logs in the center of the square was now complete. It was lit into a bonfire, raging in the brilliant afternoon. The body of a youth was then carried from a home to the edge of the bonfire. (Thirty-four years after my visit, I would learn that a great effort was traditionally made to ensure that the restless ghosts of the recently deceased were placated so they didn't cause illnesses or create imbalances.)

All voices in the village were hushed, including those of us non-villager witnesses. Unlike nearly every other resident, this teenager was dressed in Western pants and a T-shirt. One by one, family members and friends carried a T-shirt to the bonfire. Each shirt was slipped onto the youth, now wearing six or eight. The body was gently lifted up and placed on the burning fire. The ashes of the deceased, Jos told me, would be poured into an urn and buried, first by the men's house and later, for a longer time, in front of the women's house.

The youth will thus be long remembered, like those of all ages from past generations of the Dani people.

THE SLOW
GOODBYES

Lomas the Traveler

By Poet and Writer Andy Anderson

Lomas felt more comfortable traveling
somewhere there other than here.
He figured that travel is better than a rocking chair.
Off, with a small backpack with bare essentials:
 no anchors
  no dog
   no wife
    no job
     no driving machine.
The sea beckons him.
The rolling savage hills beckon.
The narrow roads hugging cliff sides beckon.
Quaint hidden villages beckon.
Follow the rainbow to its end
because it has no end to the pot of gold,
just yellow gold road beneath his feet.
Lomas would not be a deep-rooted dandelion
but rather the feathery dandelion seeds
to ride the breezes
with the soaring hawks that seldom land.
The voices call:
Spanish,
 Quechua
  Mayan
   Creole

The tastes tease:
turmeric
  cilantro
   nutmeg
    sage
The potent threaten:
mescal,
  tequila,
   Calaveras
    Monte Cristo cigar.
After years and years of cots & mosquitoes
Lomas the Traveler refuses to retire
although much more difficult now with a walker.
But wait! For he's spotted a new rainbow
just beyond the next village.

                      Dedicated to Thomas Mattson, wherever you are. ANDY

The Slow Goodbyes of Lomas the Traveler

JANUARY 1, 2020

Absorbing a treasurable poem fresh from the mind of poet Andy Anderson is worth the wait. In this poem, Lomas the Traveler is forever moving toward "a new rainbow just beyond the next village." I now find myself drifting into the personage of Lomas the Traveler surprisingly often. Lomas, using a walker, reminisces—and dreams on, too.

One day, awaking from his trance-like state, Lomas discovers his walker is nowhere to be seen. He is still *Thomas*. It's a rush to realize that the stage of life with a walker, though rewarding in many important ways, has not yet arrived. Thomas makes a promise to himself: "Being more capable than I thought, I'll dedicate the coming year to global travel, and to writing up my adventures which *few if any have heard about*."

He hopes to introduce you to new characters within the next year. They speak Swahili and Maasai, Thai and Cambodian, Bhutanese and Burmese, Hopi and Navaho. Their communities include Battambang and Phnom Penh, Rangoon and Mandalay, Saguache and Tahlequah, Acoma Pueblo and Zuni Pueblo. These stories must be written before they can be read, or perhaps *listened* to on a device you already own.

Thomas the Traveler jumps up. He's determined to walk toward a new rainbow just beyond the next village. Untold stories, all so tantalizing, are churning in his head. Many days, he'll walk at a brisk pace toward that next rainbow and then take the time to sit down and get all the words just right. Words he hopes you'll love to read a year from now. And, if you have one of those devices, words you'll perhaps love to hear as well.

To continue following Tom's travels
and adventures visit his website

TomsGlobe.com

CPSIA information can be obtained
at www.ICGtesting.com
Printed in the USA
FSHW011208270120